# CRICKET

Six of the Best

# CRICKET

Six of the Best

Bob Willis

with Pat Gibson

Hodder & Stoughton

First published in Great Britain in 1996 by
Hodder and Stoughton
a division of Hodder Headline PLC

10 9 8 7 6 5 4 3 2 1

A CIP catalogue record for this title is available from
the British Library

ISBN 0 340 67237 4

Printed and bound in Great Britain by
Mackays of Chatham PLC

Hodder and Stoughton Ltd
A Division of Hodder Headline PLC
338 Euston Road
London NW1 3BH

# ACKNOWLEDGEMENTS

I would particularly like to thank Pat Gibson for helping me make my selections by way of his probing questions and friendly argument and for his help with the preparation of the manuscript. Thanks also to Roddy Bloomfield, my publisher, for asking me to write this book, and to Patrick Eagar for providing the excellent photographs.

# CONTENTS

# FOREWORD

Bob Willis never got the credit he deserved for making me the most miserable man in the world . . .

Headingley, 21 July 1981. I remember the date and the details as vividly as other Australians recall Anzac Day or English kids are schooled to remember 1066 and all that. The day when we lost a Test match we couldn't lose, the day when R.G.D. Willis took 8 for 43 with eyes like pinholes in the snow and England won an Ashes Test after following on.

It went down in history as Ian Botham's match and no wonder, since he lifted England off the floor and put them in a position where they could actually think about winning the game. Botham gets all the wraps and I can't begrudge him that. But I hope history doesn't forget who actually bowled England to victory on that amazing last day. I know I never shall. I can still see him now, steaming in down the hill, arms waving in all directions like a demented spider. A man possessed if ever there was one. Take a careful look at the replays some time and take particular note of Bob's eyes; they were absolutely spinning. If I wanted to inflict a nightmare on myself I'd nod off to sleep thinking about Bob Willis's eyes at Headingley that day.

It was the worst moment of my cricket life and I've never denied the fact. It helped motivate me in later years and it was particularly satisfying to start a fabulous Ashes series in 1989 with a win at Headingley. We were expected to lose on our bogey ground, we won well and we never looked back in that series; I suspect somebody's attempt at psychology rebounded badly.

I read afterwards – and Bob confirms it in his book – that England were considering dropping him before the fateful Headingley match in 1981. Written off because of recurring injuries, no longer quick enough or motivated enough. The usual theoretical stuff. All I can say is that if he was supposed to be over the hill he came down the other side like a bloody train. Great pace, perfect length for the pitch he was bowling on. Remember he took eight-for and Australia only lost by 18 runs . . . It was one of the great bowling feats of Test history.

Bob was England's captain in Australia during the 1982–3 series and I remember how hard he worked to deny us victory in the Test at Melbourne. Thommo and I put on 70 for the last wicket and damned nearly pulled it off, but Bob's nerve held and we finally lost by three runs. A hell of a match.

Bob was a great competitor and a thinking bowler. Not one of the beef and brawn brigade who race in and let the ball go without too much idea where it's going. He was quick at his best, no doubt about that, but like all genuine bowlers he had a brain to go with his pace and fire. He was an intelligent bowler and all the more dangerous for that. And his assessment of the top players of his time, from the great batsmen he was up against to his fellow fast bowlers, from the superstar all-rounders to the beguiling spinners, makes fascinating reading.

I also remember Bob as a bloke who played cricket the right way. Hard on the field, ready to have a drink and a joke after hours. That's how Australians have always enjoyed playing the game and I never had a problem with Bob in that respect. He had a quick wit, a droll and off-beat sort of humour, which also comes across in the book. I never shared a dressing room with him, of course, but I imagine it was an interesting experience . . .

He beat the system in many ways and that is never a bad thing. The individuality and naturalness wasn't drummed out of him by an English coaching system which can be too rigid. It was a bit off-putting for opposing batsmen to see him bearing down with his long hair flowing and double-jointed limbs working in all directions. Could anybody really bowl fast and resourcefully with an action like Bob Willis? Course not. Until you look in the record books . . .

Allan Border
Brisbane 1996

# INTRODUCTION

One of the most popular pastimes for people who follow cricket is debating who are the best players of the day and how they compare with the great players of the past. They stand around in pubs and clubs, in beach bars and tea rooms, arguing about whether Botham was better than Sobers, whether Holding was faster than Larwood or whether Lara can compare with Bradman.

I do not know the answers but I do have my opinions, based on twenty-five years' involvement in Test cricket from the time I was flown to Australia as a replacement fast bowler on England's 1970–1 tour to my current role as a member of the Sky Sports television commentary team.

All cricketers are guilty of thinking that the players of their time were indisputably the best, that the next generation is never quite as good as they used to be, but has there, I wonder, ever been a richer twenty-five-year period in cricket history?

When it began, Sir Garfield Sobers, arguably the greatest cricketer of all, was still playing while Brian Lara, who was to break his Test batting record, had not yet reached his first birthday. Sunil Gavaskar was on his way to becoming one of the world's greatest opening batsmen while Sachin Tendulkar had not even been born. Not that everything has changed. Raymond Illingworth was captain of England; the 'nineties saw him back in charge as the first supremo of English cricket.

So what are we to make of it all? In every sport where performances can be measured by time or distance, records are being broken all the time, the old barriers are being pushed back, progress is obviously being made.

Does the same thing apply to cricket? Certainly in one area, where speed and athleticism are there for all to see, it does. Fielding has reached new heights with players diving around the boundary, sliding along on their knees and backsides and diving headlong into advertising boards in a way that their predecessors would not even have contemplated.

But what about batting and bowling? Are the West Indian fast bowlers the quickest the game has ever seen? Has anyone spun a cricket ball quite as much as Shane Warne? Did any of the legendary batsmen of the past hit the ball as hard as Viv Richards?

There are no answers to these questions. Only opinions. We all have our own, of course, but after fifteen years as a Test player and another ten as a commentator, I feel I am in a pretty good position to judge not just the England players but the people they have played against.

I have broken down the period into five specific eras – 1990–5, 1980–9, 1970–9 and 1970–95, analysing first the England players and then those from the rest of the world in each department of the game, and choosing my 'six of the best'. Finally I have drawn up my list of the all-time great players from England and the rest of the world in each category. Since I did not have the privilege of seeing some of them play, I have had to rely on their records and reputations to compare them with the modern players.

In addition I have listed my six best Test sides from England and the Rest of the World during my time in the game, the six most exciting Test matches, the six most humorous moments, the six most sporting gestures, and the six best nightwatchmen. The people concerned will not thank me for it but I have also included the six worst number elevens and the six most embarrassing commentators' blunders.

Perhaps you think I should be included in there somewhere, but see if you agree with my views.

# 1

# OPENING BATSMEN

## England

1990–5

1    Michael Atherton

2    Graham Gooch

3    Alec Stewart

4    Wayne Larkins

5    Hugh Morris

6    Jason Gallian

I believe that MICHAEL ATHERTON is going to become one of the all-time great opening batsmen as long as his dodgy back holds out long enough. Like so many England players, he made a tentative start to his England career when he first got into the side in 1989, although that was not altogether surprising in view of the way he was treated by his captain. He and Graham Gooch were to form one of England's most successful opening partnerships so it is ironic that I never felt that Gooch handled him as well as he might have done. It seemed strange, for example, that after being named man of the series in the one-day internationals against the West Indies in 1991, he virtually disappeared from the one-day scene for about eighteen months. It seemed strange, too, that he was left out of the Test side in India in 1992–3 even after Gooch had been taken ill. It is only since he took over the captaincy in 1993 that Atherton has really come into his own, showing great character as well as great technique in some memorable innings, particularly against the West Indies and South Africa. You can see the influence that Geoffrey Boycott has had on him in that he has learned the best of Boycott's technique. But he is also a very bright young man and he probably has more lateral thought processes than Boycott ever had. I put Atherton in the highest class.

If ever a captain tried to lead by example it was GRAHAM GOOCH, so it must have been heartbreaking for him to witness so many England batting collapses from twenty-two yards away. He could not have done much more than he did. He finished up as England's leading Test run-scorer which said as much for his endurance as his ability. It came from his own particular way of preparing himself for international cricket. He decided years ago after training with his beloved West Ham United that he was going to get himself really fit for the job and from then on he really put himself through it. He had caught the running bug in a big way and some of his training routines on tour were quite awesome. When he became captain, he sought to instil the same philosophy into his players, trying to get them to train and practise a lot harder than they had been used to doing. This had its problems with the more elderly brethren like Ian Botham and Mike Gatting, but some of the younger brigade, most notably Alec Stewart, took the Gooch regime to heart and it seemed to improve their play. If Gooch had a weakness as an opening batsman at the highest level it was against the medium pace and swing bowlers rather than the real fast men. He took a bit of pain, as he would put it, against the quicks, but it was the likes of Terry Alderman who gave him his biggest problems.

ALEC STEWART had reached something of a crossroads in his career when England went to South Africa in 1995–6. He had not been playing very much because of injuries over the previous twelve months and, when he had been playing, he had not been scoring many runs. His achievement in scoring two hundreds in the same Test match against the West Indies in Barbados in 1994 was tremendous and was seen in some quarters as confirming his status as a world-class batsman; however, that performance has to be put into context. England were 3–0 down and the series had already been lost and although people immediately inked him into the England side for the foreseeable future he was still some way behind Atherton and Gooch when it came to consistency. Having said that, he is a more instinctive player than either of them. He loves fast pitches with even bounce but his technique can be exposed when the bounce is uneven. He gets bowled out too often to be considered a great player, although when he is on form he is a terrific foil for Atherton because he keeps the scoreboard ticking along. Atherton is very much a one-run-per-over man before lunch on the first day of a Test match whereas Stewart tends to go too far the other way. He can get carried away and sometimes gets out playing extravagant strokes to balls which do not warrant such treatment.

Trying to find three more opening batsmen from the 1990–5 period who qualify for inclusion among 'six of the best' is a serious struggle and gives you some idea of the problems facing the England selectors, especially with Gooch now retired and Stewart well into his thirties. WAYNE LARKINS was always a favourite of Gooch, who took him to both the West Indies and Australia, but he never quite fulfilled his potential either at county or international level. He was basically a good back-foot player and a tremendous timer of the ball; however he just did not seem to have the nous to unravel the intricacies of opening the batting for England. He finished up as a bitter and disillusioned figure, having been sacked by Durham after scoring a hundred in his last innings for them. His attitude always seemed to be that the world was against him and he never struck me as a character who was going to make things happen.

In the circumstances, I think that HUGH MORRIS was unlucky not to win more than three Test caps – two against the West Indies, one against Sri Lanka – in 1991. Despite his achievement in scoring more runs in a season (2,276) and more centuries (10) than any Glamorgan player the previous year, he was clearly lacking what it takes to perform as an opening batsman at the highest level. However, he certainly showed immense courage in making 44 against Ambrose, Patterson and company on a lightning fast pitch at the Foster's Oval and must have been aggrieved when he was not picked for that winter's Australian tour. As it happened, he was flown out as a replacement – or a 'reinforcement' as the management called him – when Gooch was injured, but he played in only two minor games and was never seen again on the international scene.

JASON GALLIAN and Nick Knight are the latest openers to be tried by England and having seen them both against the West Indies in 1995 I thought the selectors got it right when they went for Gallian when John Crawley was injured on the South African tour. A lot of people seem to be getting excited about the left-handed Knight although I have to say that I am not a member of his fan club. Apart from the fact that the modest Jonathan Lewis kept him out of the Essex side for most of the 1994 season, Knight's technique, especially the way he moves his back foot outside leg stump and pokes his bat at the ball, looks all wrong to me. Gallian, on the other hand, strikes me as having a very good temperament although he needs to iron out his infuriating hop across the stumps against the quicker bowlers. I have talked to much better judges of batsmen than I am about this and they do not see it as a problem but I think that if a batsman is on the move from leg to off when the ball is being delivered he cannot be in the right position when it arrives.

&#42;      &#42;      ●      &#42;      &#42;

1980–9

1      Geoff Boycott

2      Graham Gooch

3      Chris Broad

4      Chris Tavare

5      Tim Robinson

6      Mike Brearley

Whatever people say about GEOFF BOYCOTT – and they say an awful lot – he was probably the greatest manufactured talent the game has seen. He had a tremendous dedication to practice and incredible patience at the crease, both of which combined to make him the most dependable opening batsman of his time. I have to admit that when I first got into the England side and we won the toss and chose to bat on a true pitch, we really did feel that he was going to be there all day. Apart from when he was opening with John Edrich, one did not think that way about too many subsequent England openers. Boycott was not around for much of the 'eighties but he certainly made his presence felt, first by involving himself in setting up Graham Gooch's 'rebel' tour of South Africa in 1981–2, which had such an impact on English cricket, and then by influencing a new generation of England batsmen. He and Gooch had been very close even before that and his dedication was to rub off on other 'disciples' like Atherton and Stewart.

From a technical point of view, Boycott had one of the best defensive methods there has ever been. He simply tried to eliminate any possible chance of getting out before he started to think about scoring runs. As we have seen with Atherton in more recent times, occupation of the crease is just as important as beating the ball to the boundary in the context of the five-day game. Early in his career, Boycott had a much-publicised problem against left-arm over-the-wicket spin bowlers, most notably Garfield Sobers, but on one famous occasion at Old Trafford in 1974 the Indian, Eknath Solkar, got him out in the gloaming at about twenty minutes past seven. It was the first series in which the extra hour had been added to make up for time lost to stoppages and Geoffrey was not best pleased.

The following winter, he was accused of not wanting to face Dennis Lillee and Jeff Thomson when he withdrew from the Australian tour because he felt that 'he could not do justice to himself'. I think that was a heap of rubbish. The fact is that GB had a few strange ideas going around in his head at the time. He had set his heart on captaining England when Raymond Illingworth lost the job at the end of the 1973 season, but the selectors bowled him a bit of a googly by naming Mike Denness instead for the tour of the West Indies. Ironically, Boycott and the other contender, Tony Greig, then turned in performances in the deciding Test in Trinidad which kept Denness in the position. Boycott did actually go on to captain England on four occasions – once in Pakistan and three times in New Zealand – after Mike Brearley broke his arm in a practice match in Karachi but I do not think he was ever destined to do the job on a regular basis. As we saw at Yorkshire, he did not really have a great capacity for leadership. The beginning of the end for Boycott came on the dreadful tour of India under Keith Fletcher in 1981–2. He did not enjoy it, he was never really in the right frame of mind to play, and a fortnight after passing Sobers's record of 8,032 Test runs he went home on the grounds of 'physical and mental tiredness'. This, coupled with his involvement in the 'rebel' tour, signalled the end of an extraordinary career.

CHRIS BROAD was another complex character who, like

Boycott, had a capacity for making headlines for the wrong reasons. He blotted his copybook on Mike Gatting's infamous tour of Pakistan in 1987-8 by refusing to leave the crease after being given out caught behind and not long afterwards besmirched Australia's bicentennial Test by childishly flattening his leg stump after being bowled off his body. Such petulance was a great pity because overall and with a mixture of opening partners he performed very creditably for England, particularly against the Australians. He had a lot going for him as an opening batsman – his left-handedness, stickability, phlegmatic temperament (most of the time, anyway) and some very productive shots, mainly square on both sides of the wicket to balls which were off target. He was seen at his best in Australia in 1986-7 when he really was a force to be reckoned with. Australia were at a low ebb at the time but Broad was certainly in punishing form. He scored three hundreds in three successive Tests and finished up with 487 runs in the series, added another 559 in the two one-day international competitions and walked off with the International Player of the Season award. Again like Boycott, he had aspirations to captaincy, but he was thwarted at every turn as he flitted from Gloucestershire to Nottinghamshire and back again. A reputation for not being too good against spin had led to his exclusion from David Gower's tour of India in 1984-5 and people thought of him as a bit of a camel in the field, especially towards the end of his career. This was palpably unfair because he was obviously affected by severe arthritis of the hip which was to bring his playing days to a premature close.

CHRIS TAVARE was not everyone's cup of tea as an opening batsman but, having played a lot of Test cricket with him at the height of my own powers, I have to confess that I was always a fan of his. For one reason or another, we had a fair number of dashers in the middle-order during the second half of my career, players like Gower, Lamb, Botham and, to a slightly lesser extent, Randall, and we needed someone a bit more adhesive either opening the batting or going in at number three. Tavare was that man even though he did take things to extremes and turn himself into a bit of a tortoise. He was a bright lad, an Oxbridge product, so there were no problems with the long-term concentration when it came to occupying the crease but he got into the habit of patting half-volleys back to the bowler. In the end he could have batted all day, or the best part of it, yet the bowlers never felt tired because he was just not dominating enough. The strange thing about that was that he could be dominating in one-day cricket, not just for Kent and

Somerset, the two counties he represented so well, but also for England. I do not know what influenced his peculiar style in Test cricket but I have a couple of theories. It could be that he was so upset at being left out of the side, as so many batsmen are after modest performances at the start of their England careers, that it made him all the more determined. Or it may be that he went back to Kent and people like Alan Knott, Bob Woolmer and Derek Underwood instilled in him how important it was to stay out in the middle if you want to score runs in Test cricket. If that was the case, he certainly took it to the ultimate degree. Not that I was complaining about that when I was captain in Australia in 1982–3. Our other two opening batsmen, Graeme Fowler and Geoff Cook, had a pretty wretched time and I remember how thankful I was to have Tav there to try and hold things together.

My main recollection of TIM ROBINSON is of him being trapped like a rabbit in the headlights on David Gower's ill-fated tour of the Caribbean in 1985–6. The West Indian fast bowlers lost no time in sorting him out, usually by going round the wicket and pounding the ball into the middle of the pitch whereupon Robinson would provide catching practice for the slip and gully fielders. Until then, however, he had an imposing Test record, having scored 934 runs in eleven innings in his first year of Test cricket. He batted with tremendous aplomb on his first tour to India under David Gower in 1984–5, scoring 160 at Delhi in only his second Test, and then scored two more big hundreds against a poor Australian side at home the following summer. That was the great thing about him. If he did get in, he usually made it count. Ten years on, he was still churning out the runs for Nottinghamshire but, to all intents and purposes, that West Indian tour had finished him off as an international player and meant that he would never go down as a really top-class batsman.

My sixth choice from the 'eighties could never be put in that category, either, but I have included MIKE BREARLEY because of the influence he had on the England side in general and Ian Botham in particular. He is best remembered for the way he returned to mastermind the Ashes triumph over Australia in 1981 in one of the most famous Test series ever played, yet England were actually thinking of him as an opening batsman as far back as 1964–5 when he went to South Africa under M. J. K. Smith. Not long after that, he disappeared from the game altogether to follow an academic career and it was quite remarkable that he came back to play Test cricket at all. He first got into the England side against the West Indies in 1976 but it was soon pretty obvious that he did not have what it takes to be an opening batsman at international level. There were times in the 'seventies when England even had to play seven specialist batsmen, Brearley included, to paper over the cracks. Looking back, it is difficult to think of one Brearley innings which stands out in the memory. Whenever he survived the new ball and seemed to have got himself set, he would just get out for no apparent reason, usually in defensive mode. The fact that he played in as many Test matches as he did (thirty-nine) just goes to show how important powers of intellect can be in the game of cricket. I have already mentioned Atherton and Tavare in this context and I do think it helps, particularly when it comes to concentrating for long periods of time. One of the most valid criticisms of English players over the years – and not just in cricket but in other sports as well – is that they seem to have a very low boredom threshold. I think the more intelligent a player is, the better use he makes of his spare time, the more likely he is to be able to concentrate on the job in hand. Batting, and particularly opening the batting, is as much about being mentally alert as being physically fit.

*          *          ●          *          *

1970–9

1    Geoff Boycott

2    John Edrich

3    Dennis Amiss

4    Brian Luckhurst

5    David Lloyd

6    Barry Wood

The 'seventies began with three of England's best post-war opening batsmen playing leading roles on Raymond Illingworth's Ashes-winning tour of Australia. I have already said quite a lot about GEOFF BOYCOTT, but that 1970-1 series, in which he scored 657 runs, probably saw him at his best. He was quite happy to practise all day as long as he could find someone to bowl at him, and he was often quite capable of batting all day in the Test matches as well on some very good, even-paced Australian wickets. The only exception was Sydney and it was there that his tour ended when he had his arm broken by Graham McKenzie in a meaningless match against Western Australia, that season's Gillette Cup holders.

Boycott's most enduring partner was JOHN EDRICH, although he went in first wicket down for most of that tour to allow Brian Luckhurst to open. Not that it made much difference to Edrich. Phlegmatic is the word that springs to mind in describing him. He had a terrific temperament for the job and did not even seem flustered when he and Brian Close were being terrorised by the frightening pace of the West Indian fast bowlers on a corrugated pitch at Old Trafford in 1976. Edrich was still as brave as they come but his best years were behind him by then. He had played the first of his seventy-seven Tests against the West Indies in 1963 and throughout his England career he was thoroughly reliable. I was not around to see his 310 not out against New Zealand at Headingley in 1965 although I saw enough of him after that to know that he was very capable of going on to make really big scores once he had got into three figures. He had the advantage – and I do think it is an advantage for an opening batsman – of being a left-hander. It is a real problem for opening bowlers to vary their line for right-handers and left-handers because any swing you get seems to be accentuated when you keep having to adjust. Edrich epitomised a classic cliché in that he really did know exactly where his off stump was, with the result that he was very rarely bowled out. He was a good runner as well and did not have as many problems with Boycott as some of his other partners did. I also had good reason to be grateful to John Edrich since he was responsible for my inclusion on the 1970-1 tour. Ray Illingworth had hardly seen me bowl and it was very much on John's recommendation that I was called up as a replacement when Alan Ward had to return home injured.

BRIAN LUCKHURST also made his Test debut on that tour and he immediately looked the part even though he had had to wait until he was nearly thirty-two for his opportunity. He was not in the same class as either Boycott or Edrich but he was a very solid opening batsman and his technique was only really exposed by the faster wickets and extra bounce we encountered in Australia four years later, particularly at Brisbane and Perth. Messrs Lillee and Thomson caused him all kinds of problems then but he was not alone in that. Luckhurst was one of three England batsmen who suffered broken bones.

This was in the days before batsmen began to put on helmets for extra protection and it is probably no coincidence that it was another of the casualties of that tour, DENNIS AMISS, who was among the first to wear one. He had been hit on the head by Michael Holding on his way to scoring a double century on a particularly flat pitch at The Oval in 1976, and when he went off to join Kerry Packer's World Series Cricket the following year he took to wearing what was almost a motorcyclist's crash helmet. He had started his England career in 1966 against the West Indies and they were to come to respect him as a formidable opponent, especially after he switched to opening the batting in the early 'seventies. He was one of the few England batsmen to make runs consistently against them in the Caribbean in 1973–4 and I remember being at the other end when he finished with 262 not out in the Jamaica Test. Like a lot of batsmen, Dennis was at his best when the ball was not bouncing too much. He was not so happy when it was lifting and leaving him around off stump, and he was exposed on the 1974–5 Australian tour – but, then, who wasn't? Above all, he was a very dogged campaigner as he showed in 1978 when he was almost an outcast in the Warwickshire dressing room on his return from his Packer adventure. It was remarkable how entrenched people's positions had become over Packer's activities and the perceived threat to the county game but Dennis just got on with his job like he always did.

DAVID LLOYD made an almost immediate impact as an England opening batsman by scoring 214 not out in only his second Test at Edgbaston in 1974 and although he did it against a fairly innocuous attack he would probably prefer me to dwell on that rather than on his experience in Australia the following winter. Sorry, Bumble, there are some things you simply cannot forget. He just did not find Australia to his liking, either on or off the field. I remember him being very homesick on that tour and when Jeff Thomson compounded his misery by hitting him full in the box in the Perth Test one could not help feeling sorry for him. He had opened with Colin Cowdrey, who had just been added to the squad because both Edrich and Luckhurst were injured, and I will never forget the electrifying sight of Lillee and Thomson roaring in at full cry on that fast, bouncy pitch. Nor will I forget the colour of poor Bumble's face as he was helped from the field. It was ashen. He was never quite the same again, which was a shame because he was a goodish player and, though not having the technique of an Edrich, quite a classy one, too.

Lloyd's Lancashire partner, BARRY WOOD, could probably count himself lucky that he was not called up as a replacement on that tour until the team had moved on to New Zealand, although he might have done a bit better against the quick bowlers than he had done against the spinners in India the previous winter. He was a good-looking player but while he and Lloyd did a good job opening for Lancashire you could not say that either of them was really at home playing at the highest level. One-day cricket was a different matter. Here Woody was in his element with his medium-pace bowling as valuable as his batting, as no fewer than seventeen man-of-the-match awards testify.

\*　　\*　　●　　\*　　\*

1970–95

1　Geoff Boycott
2　Graham Gooch
3　John Edrich
4　Michael Atherton
5　Dennis Amiss
6　Alec Stewart

All-time

1    Sir Jack Hobbs
2    Sir Len Hutton
3    Geoff Boycott
4    Graham Gooch
5    Herbert Sutcliffe
6    Cyril Washbrook

It is difficult to make comparisons between players who appeared so many years apart, because we are not too familiar with the bowling attacks and field placings they were up against; however, from all that I have heard and read BOYCOTT and GOOCH are the only opening batsmen from my generation who qualify for my 'six of the best'.

The top two must be JACK HOBBS and LEN HUTTON, who were both knighted for their services to the game, and I think we need look no further than their most respected partners, HERBERT SUTCLIFFE and CYRIL WASHBROOK, to complete the list.

# Rest of the World

1990–5

1   Mark Taylor

2   Desmond Haynes

3   Michael Slater

4   Gordon Greenidge

5   Geoff Marsh

6   Aamir Sohail

As 1995 drew to a close, there was no denying the fact that Australia had become the undisputed champions of Test match cricket, and one of the major reasons for that was the emergence of MARK TAYLOR and Michael Slater as the best pair of opening batsmen in the world. We first came across Tubby Taylor in England in 1989 when Australia surprised us by splitting the long-standing and totally reliable opening pairing of Geoff Marsh and David Boon to give him his chance. Their manager, Bob Simpson, was convinced that there was nothing better than a right-hander and a left-hander batting together and his judgment was vindicated as Marsh and Taylor went on to form a prolific association. Taylor began with 136 in his first Ashes Test at Headingley and proceeded to score fifty or more in every match of the series, including a monumental 219 at Trent Bridge where he and Marsh put on 329, a record opening stand in England–Australia Tests. Nothing has happened since to alter my opinion that Taylor is a very high-class player indeed. He did have a slight hiccup when he first took over the captaincy from Allan Border in Pakistan in 1994 but he quickly put that behind him against England that winter and seems to be going from strength to strength. He has the advantage of being a left-hander, which I have already talked about, and, like so many left-handers, he is a very strong onside player, both off his pads and off his hips when the ball is new and bouncing a bit more. He does not really get his offside shots going until later in his innings – unless someone gives him a loose, short ball which he is quick to cut – but although his partner always seems to be scoring faster than he is, he keeps the scoreboard moving pretty well himself. He is a good player of spin as well, and while that is not the first thing you look for in an opening batsman, it has to be taken into consideration in assessing a player's all-round ability.

His first partner, GEOFF MARSH, also had a good record against England but his figures against the other Test-playing countries do not warrant his being higher than fifth on my list for the early 'nineties. He was a pretty good player, though, and it was his rapport with Taylor in 1989 that first gave Australia an ascendancy over England which they have held ever since. Marsh was competent rather than exciting until it came to running between the wickets, where he was very good indeed and built up an excellent understanding with Taylor. There were the occasional mix-ups but they never resulted in the kind of post mortems we used to see whenever Geoffrey Boycott was involved in a run-out.

Marsh and Taylor set the standard in that respect and now Taylor and MICHAEL SLATER have almost turned it into an art form. Picking up quick singles in Test match cricket, especially at the start of an innings, really infuriates the bowlers and Taylor and Slater are usually out of their blocks from the word go. Slater does not hang about in any other aspect of his batting, either. Just as Australia had separated Marsh and Boon to give Taylor his chance in 1989, so they split up Taylor and Marsh to launch Slater on an unsuspecting English public. He made 58 on his debut at Trent Bridge and when he followed that with a century at Lord's, which he celebrated by kissing the badge on his helmet, it was clear that he was a very rare talent indeed. He has been like a breath of fresh air, really, in that he is one of the few opening batsmen who will treat every ball on its merits – even if it is the first one bowled in a Test match. His flamboyance has been his undoing once or twice but I have to say that for a player who is still in the early stages of his career he is one of the most exciting prospects world cricket has seen for a long time.

Until the arrival of first Taylor and then Slater, there was no one to challenge GORDON GREENIDGE and Desmond Haynes as the best pair of opening batsmen in the world. I knew Gordon only too well, having first crossed swords with him in a second-team match between Surrey and Hampshire at Guildford way back in 1969. He hit me into Woodbridge Road during that game and he went on to hit many other top-class bowlers out of the ground for the next twenty years and more. He never lost his attacking instincts but he benefited enormously from batting with the great Barry Richards (about whom more later) during the early days of his career with Hampshire and I am sure this helped to convert him from being something of a Flash Harry into the complete opening batsman. He was to score nineteen Test centuries, but one innings in particular sticks in my mind. It was at Lord's in 1984 when he hit 214 not out as the West Indies made light work of a victory target of 342. Gordon was still going strong into the 'nineties when a somewhat arbitrary decision by the West Indian selectors brought his international career to an abrupt halt. Like a lot of West Indian players before him, he left with a sour taste in his mouth, which was not altogether surprising. The selectors felt that it was time to introduce some younger blood, but he was clearly still a better player than one or two of his successors will ever be.

The first of his two remarkable partners was Roy Fredericks, who we will come to later; the second, DESMOND HAYNES, who was also a sadly disillusioned figure when he left the international scene in 1995. The selectors had insisted on him playing for Barbados in all the Red Stripe Cup matches prior to the series against Australia and when he got back late from playing in South Africa they left him out of the side. Haynes responded with legal action but when they did not pick him for the subsequent tour to England it was obvious that his career was over. Again they seemed to have cut off their nose to spite their face because he would have been a far better partner for the emerging Sherwin Campbell than either Carl Hooper or Stuart Williams. Haynes was already a world-class player when he went to play for Middlesex in 1989 but, like Greenidge, he seemed to benefit from the experience of playing county cricket. He made runs against all kinds of bowling in all sorts of conditions and although I always fancied getting both him and Greenidge lbw early on – because, in common with all the great players, their first movement was back and across – I knew that if we didn't remove them quickly we were in for a long day in the field. What made it all the more frustrating was that when they were not crashing the ball to the boundary they would often just drop it at their feet and pinch quick singles, such was their great understanding.

I guess it is a reflection of the dominance of the West Indies and Australia in Test cricket over the period that I am scratching around for a sixth opening batsman, but I have gone for AAMIR

SOHAIL if only because he has survived the strange goings-on in Pakistan cricket without any apparent deterioration in his output. He is quite an unorthodox, left-handed opener but he can be highly effective, as he showed by scoring 205 in only his second Test match against England at Old Trafford in 1992.

\*          \*          ●          \*          \*

1980–9

1   Sunil Gavaskar

2   Gordon Greenidge

3   Desmond Haynes

4   Mark Taylor

5   John Wright

6   Mudassar Nazar

This period saw GORDON GREENIDGE and DESMOND HAYNES at the peak of their careers, and with MARK TAYLOR starting his career so spectacularly I am left with only three spots to fill.

Pride of place must go to SUNIL GAVASKAR, the little master from India, who had started his Test career back in 1970 and just carried on piling up the runs until 1987 when he signed off with a Test century for the Rest of the World in the MCC bicentenary match at Lord's. He had scored his runs, more than 10,000 of them, including thirty-four centuries, all over the world, but, in recent times at any rate, I think it is a batsman's record against the West Indies which tells you how good he really was. Suffice it to say that Gavaskar made thirteen of his hundreds against them, seven in the Caribbean. He was only just over 5ft 4in tall but he used his stature, or in his case his lack of it, to his advantage. He was a brilliant leaver of the ball on height early in his innings which meant that if a fast bowler banged the ball in short he would just sway out of the way and let it go through to the wicketkeeper, often over the top of the stumps. Fast bowlers like me had to make a major adjustment when bowling to him and pitch the ball the best part of a yard further up than we would do against a taller batsman. He was also a terrific player of spin bowling which was bread and butter to him since he had developed his technique on the turning pitches of the subcontinent. All things considered, he was a wonderful all-round opening batsman and it was fascinating to go to the World Masters Series in Bombay in 1995 and discover that he had lost very little of his ability. It was such a shame that a pulled hamstring prevented him from gracing the final against the West Indies and showing us what he could do against the likes of Joel Garner and Sylvester Clarke.

There is no shortage of candidates for the other two vacancies, among them Kepler Wessels, who began his Test career with Australia before going on to captain his native South Africa, the Sri Lankan, Sidath Wettimuny, who made 190 against England at Lord's in 1984, and Krishnamachari Srikkanth, the swashbuckling Indian opener. My next choice, though, is JOHN WRIGHT who did sterling work for New Zealand, particularly in the latter part of his career when he was not only opening the batting but also carrying the burden of captaining what was a very weak Test side indeed. Once Richard Hadlee retired and Martin Crowe's appearances became more and more infrequent through injury, Wright was the only player of any real class they had left. He soldiered on manfully and always gave a good account of himself, whether he was playing for New Zealand or Derbyshire, the county he served faithfully for many years. I remember many personal duels with him, especially one at Wellington in the first Test of the 1977–8 series when New Zealand beat England for the first time. Wright was making his Test debut and I got him out first ball, caught behind by Bob Taylor, diving in front of second slip. The New Zealand umpire, as was their wont, said 'not out' and Wright went on to make a crucial 55 in a low-scoring game. There were plenty of occasions after that, however, when he did not need such assistance and I was always glad to see the back of him. Indeed when he and his fellow left-hander, Bruce Edgar, were opening the batting for New Zealand, I did not like it all. I had enjoyed bowling to left-handers early in my career, but later on when I had achieved greater control and the ability to make the ball leave the right-handers, I much preferred bowling to them.

Earlier in that winter of 1977–8, I had the dubious pleasure of bowling to MUDASSAR NAZAR in the Gaddafi Stadium, Lahore, while he was scoring a hundred in nine hours twenty minutes, the slowest in Test history. It seemed a pretty meaningless pastime in a pretty meaningless Test in a pretty meaningless series, apart from the kerfuffle before the last Test when we heard that Kerry Packer was about to release his Pakistani players from World Series Cricket and let them play against us. We did not think that this was the right thing to do and there was even talk of a strike before the idea was dropped. It was an indication of the pressure, not least political pressure, the Pakistanis were under to win that series and I think players like Mudassar, who was only just starting his career, suffered from it. He was to become a much more forceful player than that Lahore innings had suggested and averaged 82 on the 1982 England tour when he and the accomplished Mohsin Khan formed an opening partnership of real quality.

\*          \*          ●          \*          \*

1970–9

1   Barry Richards

2   Sunil Gavaskar

3   Roy Fredericks

4   Lawrence Rowe/Gordon Greenidge

5   Glenn Turner

6   Majid Khan

One of the pitfalls of an exercise like this is that we tend to think that the best players of our time were the best of all time, but I have to say that I believe my six best opening batsmen from the 'seventies – or seven since I have cheated a little for reasons which I will explain – were all players of the highest quality.

At the top of my list is BARRY RICHARDS who cannot really be called the greatest in Test match terms as he played in only four matches because of South Africa's isolation from international cricket throughout most of his career, but he was certainly the most elegantly gifted batsman I have ever seen. He always looked at ease in his lovely, upright stance, unruffled in his classical, back-foot defensive technique and unhurried in his majestic strokeplay. He was not a particularly powerful man, relying very much on timing and placement, but he really was a destructive batsman and it is one of the travesties of cricket history that his skills were not seen by more people around the world. Hampshire spectators were privileged to be able to watch him for nine seasons in county cricket and South Australians could hardly believe their eyes when he went to play for them in 1970–1. He scored more than 1,500 runs that winter, averaging 109 and hitting 356 against Western Australia, 325 of them in one day. Twenty-five years later I saw him playing in the World Masters Series in Bombay and he still looked a magnificent player. The style, the elegance, the majestic cover drive, they were all undiminished.

Great players come in all shapes and sizes and a complete contrast was provided by ROY FREDERICKS, the tough little left-hander from Guyana who for a period in the 'seventies I rated third only to Richards and the aforementioned SUNIL GAVASKAR among the world's best opening batsmen. While Richards seemed to caress the ball, Fredericks really blasted it and I do not need reminding about the 1976 Headingley Test when he and Gordon Greenidge scored 149 before lunch against Alan Ward, John Snow and myself. Like most left-handers, he was also very good at flicking the ball away off his hip and legs and he was quite prepared to have a go at the first ball of the match. He did it, memorably, in the first World Cup Final at Lord's in 1975 when he hooked Lillee over the ropes at long leg only to discover that he had trodden on his stumps in the process. He made the Australians pay for that at Perth the following winter when he never put a foot wrong in what was acclaimed as one of the greatest of all innings – 169 off 145 balls against Lillee, Thomson, Gilmour and Walker on the fastest pitch in the world. 'Freddo' was a familiar figure through playing county cricket for Glamorgan but we saw him in a different guise in the Caribbean in 1980 when as Comrade Fredericks he was an adviser to the Guyanese government which would not accept Robin Jackman as my replacement because of his South African connections.

When we first saw LAWRENCE ROWE opening with

Fredericks in the West Indies in 1974 we all thought that he was going to become one of the best players in the history of the game – which is why I have bracketed him with GORDON GREENIDGE who was soon to take over from him and almost steal his inheritance. Rowe, who had achieved the unique distinction of scoring a century and a double century on his Test debut against New Zealand two years earlier, was magnificent in that series, especially when he was scoring 302 against us in the Barbados Test. There were so many spectators wanting to see him bat on the third morning that we had to climb over the wall at the Kensington Oval to get into the ground and I remember thinking to myself: 'What on earth am I doing this for just so that I can bowl at Lawrence Rowe again?' He looked a superb player yet for one reason or another he was never to have anything like the same success abroad. He had eye trouble, injuries and, strangest of all during his two miserable seasons with Derbyshire, an allergy to grass which must have been quite a disadvantage on their green wickets. Eventually he led a rebel West Indian tour to South Africa which did not exactly improve his standing in his native Jamaica and he was never quite the same again. For a short period of time, however, he was one of the most classical opening batsmen in the world.

I have to confess that I never really got on with GLENN TURNER but I must also concede that he was an opening batsman of genuine quality. If his record of 103 first-class centuries is not proof enough, it is endorsed by his achievements in the Caribbean where he scored four double centuries on one tour. I was involved in a little fracas with him during a Worcestershire–Warwickshire match when he intimated to the umpires that I was bowling too many short balls at him by making a big show of sending for a helmet. I am happy to say that I got him out lbw a few balls later although he certainly got his own back when we went back in 1982. He not only scored his hundredth hundred against us but went on to make 311 in the day! He had been a very limited player early in his career, probably as a result of the coaching he received from Billy Ibadulla, who was a pretty dour opening batsman himself, and could hardly hit the ball off the square. He benefited greatly from two major developments in the game. One was the introduction of one-day cricket which made him much more positive in his pursuit of runs and certainly enhanced his Test match performances. The other was the brilliant bat-making skill of Duncan Fearnley. Glenn was not a particularly strong man, although he finished up playing with quite a heavy bat. It was so beautifully balanced that he would control it easily by holding it right at the top of the handle.

Finally I come to the sartorially elegant MAJID KHAN, resplendent in his dirty, floppy gardener's hat and yellowing buckskin pads which somehow seemed to reflect his outlook on cricket. We knew that he was a quality player from his early days at Cambridge University but he was a very complex character and one suspected that his mind was not always on the job. He played at a time when Pakistan had a very strong batting side which should have produced more victories than it did, and certainly when he was playing for Glamorgan you never knew whether he was going to strike the first ball for four or slog it straight up into the air. At his best, though, he was a high-class performer and I well remember bowling to him at The Oval in 1974. The ploy, hatched by our captain, Mike Denness, and his senior players, was to bounce him out. He made 98 before lunch as he dispatched my non-bouncing bouncers – i.e. long hops – to all parts of SE11.

\* \* ● \* \*

1970–95

1   Sunil Gavaskar

2   Gordon Greenidge

3   Mark Taylor

4   Barry Richards

5   Desmond Haynes

6   Glenn Turner

All-time

1    Sunil Gavaskar

2    Gordon Greenidge

3    Bill Ponsford

4    Hanif Mohammad

5    Arthur Morris

6    Barry Richards

I cannot believe that there has been a better all-round opening batsman than SUNIL GAVASKAR or a more punishing one than GORDON GREENIDGE and I have to include BARRY RICHARDS in my 'six of the best', but I have had to delve into the history books for the other three. HANIF MOHAMMAD, who first played for Pakistan when he was seventeen and went on to become a national hero, once held the records for the highest Test score (337) and the highest first-class score (499), which now belong to Brian Lara, and I have it on the authority of Sir Donald Bradman and Alec Bedser that BILL PONSFORD and ARTHUR MORRIS were the greatest of all Australian opening batsmen. Their word is good enough for me.

# 2

# MIDDLE-ORDER BATSMEN

## England

1990–5

1    Graham Thorpe

2    Robin Smith

3    Allan Lamb

4    Graeme Hick

5    David Gower

6    Mike Gatting

The early 'nineties brought the last hurrahs in the careers of David Gower, Allan Lamb and Mike Gatting, the three batsmen who, in their richly contrasting styles, had dominated England's middle-order for well over a decade.

DAVID GOWER's most glorious days were behind him by now although he was still good enough to score two centuries on Graham Gooch's 1990–1 tour of Australia. Unfortunately the powers-that-be took more account of his unscheduled flight in a Tiger Moth and when he was left out of the 1992–3 tour of India – a decision which led to an extraordinary meeting of the MCC to debate the competence or otherwise of the selectors – it was clear that his Test career was over. It was a pity that it had to end that way, because from the moment he dispatched his first ball in Test cricket for four he had been an adornment to the game, easily the best middle-order batsman of his generation and, to my mind, one of the finest England have ever had. His detractors often accused him of being too flashy, playing and missing a lot outside the off stump and getting a fair number of edges early in his innings, but his record surely speaks for itself. He is England's second highest Test run scorer after Graham Gooch with 8,231, including eighteen centuries, and I prefer to remember him as a beautifully elegant left-hander, standing up on tiptoe to force the ball through the offside or getting well down the pitch to take on the spin bowlers. I well remember his regal entry against Pakistan at Edgbaston in 1974 when he pulled that first delivery (admittedly, a nice, juicy long hop from Liaqat Ali) almost nonchalantly for four; I remember, too, his first Test century at Perth on the 1978–9 tour of Australia and his last at Sydney in 1991 – he was as popular down under as he was in England and it was received with rapturous applause.

I suppose we all have our own ways of assessing players and I have to say that I was never a great MIKE GATTING fan. It took him an awfully long time to get going in Test match cricket after he had been picked for the first time on the 1977–8 tour of Pakistan and New Zealand when he was only twenty. Like so many debutants, he had a rough baptism on his debut (Karachi is not the kind of place where you feel immediately at home), but that does not explain why it should have taken him seven years and fifty-four innings to make his first Test century. He was a compact player and obviously capable of playing commanding innings, although he was very vulnerable early on against top-class bowling. He never seemed to be quite sure where his off stump was and this resulted in him being trapped lbw or bowled when he was not offering a shot far more often than he should have been. Once he did get under way, he scored more than 1,000 runs in eleven Tests. His run of success came to a painful halt in the Caribbean in 1986 when he had his nose smashed by Malcolm Marshall. I was on the scene within seconds of it happening and it was a very unpleasant sight indeed. Not only were there bits of bone in the ball but there was quite a large chunk of his nose lying on the pitch and claret all over the place. Most of us thought that his tour was over but Gatt obviously did not see it that way at all. He went home to have his nose rebuilt and before we knew it he was back in the Caribbean – only to have his thumb broken in the very next match. I may have doubted his ability but no one could question his courage, although some cynics might have suggested that the real purpose of his return trip was to throw his hat into the captaincy ring. David ('I'm auditioning for *Howard's Way*') Gower had not got off to a brilliant start by going on a sailing trip around the Grenadines while his lads were losing their very first match against the Windward Islands and sure enough Gatting took over the following summer. His later career was peppered with controversy, including his infamous confrontations with a Pakistani umpire and a Leicestershire barmaid, which led to his removal from the captaincy and his subsequent defection to lead the last, ill-advised 'rebel' tour of South Africa. He never really seemed to be at one with the cricketing establishment yet the people in the know, the managers of the teams, always wanted him around. It was a transparent mistake, however, to take him (and Graham Gooch, for that matter) on the tour of Australia in 1994–5. Both of them were well past their sell-by dates by then.

I had more time for ALLAN LAMB who was probably discarded a little bit too early after playing in the last of his seventy-nine Tests against Pakistan in 1992 although I have to admit that he should have finished up with a better average than 36. At times, no one, apart, perhaps, from Ian Botham, looked more dominant with the bat than he did but he was always liable to get out early. He had a habit of putting his bat well out in front of the pad and this cost him dearly as he often gave chances to slip or gully. He began his international career under my captaincy against India in 1982 and made an immediate impact on the dressing room. He was a very chirpy, effervescent character and it was a dangerous combination when the Botham–Lamb cocktail came together. Fortunately they could be equally formidable on the field and Lamby was seen at his best in 1984 when he made three successive hundreds against the daunting West Indian attack. He was hugely confident in his own ability, completely positive in his outlook, and I remember being grateful to him during a Test against New Zealand at Trent Bridge. The other selectors wanted to leave him out of the side to give a debut to David Thomas, the left-arm seamer from Surrey, but I stood up for Lamb, arguing that the pitch was not going to help pace bowling and that we needed all the batting strength we could muster. Fortunately for me, Lamby responded with a century and we went on to win the match quite comfortably.

Since the departure of those three from the international scene, it has been quite depressing watching England's middle-order in recent times although ROBIN SMITH certainly looked the part when he was taking on the West Indian fast bowlers in the early 'nineties. He is one of the few players who actually relishes the quick stuff, having spent hours and hours sharpening his reflexes in front of a bowling machine turned up to full pace back home in his native South Africa, though whether he will be quite so keen after taking a sickening blow from Ian Bishop at Old Trafford in 1995 remains to be seen. He is a devastating player off the back foot, particularly when he is hitting the ball square of the wicket on the offside. This is his speciality, although he is not afraid to play the pull shot to the bouncers. He prefers it, quite rightly, to the hook over which he has less control. He is a tremendous self-motivator, forever geeing himself up out in the middle with words like 'Come on, come on' and 'Concentrate, concentrate'. However, this has not helped him too much against the spinners, particularly Shane Warne who has given him such horrendous problems that he was left out of the 1994–5 tour of Australia.

Great things were also expected of GRAEME HICK when he made his long-awaited entry into the England side but he had a rocky start against the 1991 West Indians, Curtly Ambrose in particular, and he was always struggling against fast bowling aimed at his ribcage. Australia's Merv Hughes was quick to exploit the same weakness and I remain to be convinced that he has what it takes to succeed at the highest level. He is a great destroyer of mediocre county attacks and he is certainly a beautiful player when he gets on to the front foot to dispatch half volleys from the seamers or hit the spinners straight back over their heads. I think there are signs, too, that he is beginning to overcome his shortcomings against the quicks. He has benefited from adopting a more attacking approach and the pull he plays in front of square on the legside is a particularly attractive shot. Less attractive is the hook that has brought about his downfall when he has been trying to be positive and only succeeded in giving catches to the boundary fielders. At least he has managed to get his Test average moving up from the mid-twenties, where it had languished for far too long, towards the upper-thirties. I still think he has been a very lucky lad to have been given as many chances as he has. The England selectors seem determined to keep faith with him. Time will tell if they are right.

With Smith having his problems and Hick still struggling to assert himself, it is just as well for England that GRAHAM THORPE has made such a positive start to his Test career, so much so that he looks capable of becoming the cornerstone of the middle-order for the foreseeable future. The policy these days is to bring the young players through from the A team and it has paid off handsomely in his case. The Surrey left-hander had already been on four overseas tours so he knew a little bit about international cricket by the time he made his debut against Australia at Trent

Bridge in 1993 when he joined the select band of England batsmen who have scored a century in their first Ashes Test. He got into a lot of trouble at the start of the West Indies tour that winter by playing across the line of deliveries pitched well up to him but he learned his lesson well and I thought he was very unlucky to be left out of the side against New Zealand the following summer. He was back for the last two Test matches against South Africa in which he averaged 79 and he has since gone from strength to strength against Australia and the West Indies. He is a good workmanlike player who I rate very highly although he does have an infuriating habit of getting out between 50 and 100. Only twice on the four-teen occasions that he has made a half-century has he been able to turn it into a hundred and that is not good enough for a batsman with ambitions at the highest level. What he must concentrate on now is putting scores together in both innings of a match – and make sure that when he does get in he goes on to build major three-figure innings.

Of the other young batsmen, I like the look of John Crawley, who could be an Atherton clone after following the England captain from Manchester Grammar School to Cambridge University and into the Lancashire and England sides. Like Atherton, he seems to have the intelligence, the determination and the temperament to cope with Test match cricket. He was obvi-ously overweight when he was waddling around Australia in 1994–5 but he has made a great effort with his fitness and was probably a stone and a half lighter when an untimely injury stopped him in his tracks in South Africa the following winter. I think he will eventually establish himself in the England side, which is more than I can say for Mark Ramprakash. There is no question that he is a gifted strokemaker but he more than anybody epitomises the gulf between county and Test cricket. He clearly has some kind of mental block in the Test arena and when he failed again in South Africa he seemed to be a lost cause.

1980–9

1    David Gower

2    Allan Lamb

3    Derek Randall

4    Mike Gatting

5    Bill Athey

6    Rob Bailey

David Gower, Allan Lamb and Mike Gatting so dominated England's middle-order batting during this period that only one other player, DEREK RANDALL, made any kind of impact – and he was never the same again after he had taken a horrific blow in the mouth from Michael Holding on a dodgy pitch in Tasmania. 'Arkle', as we called him, had sprung to fame with his incredible innings of 174 in the Centenary Test at Melbourne in 1977 but I was not altogether surprised by his success. I had come across him playing for Nottinghamshire against Warwickshire very early in his career and remember thinking to myself: 'This lad can play a bit.' And so he could. He was an amazing character, outwardly bubbly but as nervous as a church mouse, and he always liked to talk to the opposition when he was batting because it helped to relax him. Some captains caught on to this and would go to the extent of telling their fielders not to say a word to him and let him stew in his own juice. Not surprisingly, he was a jumpy starter and he was certainly exposed by the best quick bowlers which is why he did not have much of a record against the West Indies. He had a very good back-foot technique, though, and playing for Nottinghamshire on Ron Allsopp's lively Trent Bridge pitches in the Rice and Hadlee years meant that he kept on improving in that area, which is so vital if a batsman is going to succeed in Test cricket. Another reason why I liked to have him in my team was because he was such an adaptable player. He was most comfortable in the middle-order but he was quite happy to open the batting if he was asked to do it. He just wanted to play for England and his commitment was never better demonstrated than in his innings of 150 at Sydney in 1978–9. The heat was searing with almost a hundred per cent humidity and both Mike Hendrick and myself had to leave the field with heat exhaustion. Arkle batted for almost ten hours in it. He was also an exceptional fielder, of course, and a terrific bloke to have around the dressing room, where his absent-mindedness was a constant source of amusement. He was quite capable of turning up at the wrong hotel or packing his shoes in his suitcase and having to travel barefoot between Melbourne and Sydney.

I am loath to include ROB BAILEY and BILL ATHEY in my 'six of the best' since neither of them could average more than 15 in Test cricket, but hardly anyone else got a look-in during the 'eighties. Bailey could consider himself unlucky in that all four of his Tests were against the West Indies and since he was basically a front-foot player the results were fairly predictable. Athey had a reasonable tour of Australia in 1986–7, although he obviously lacked what it takes to play at the highest level. So many Yorkshire players who had been brought up in the shadow of Geoffrey Boycott were given an opportunity for England and never covered themselves in glory.

\*     \*     ●     \*     \*

1970–9

1   David Gower

2   Derek Randall

3   Keith Fletcher

4   David Steele

5   Colin Cowdrey

6   John Hampshire

With England often including any three opening batsmen from Boycott, Edrich, Luckhurst, Denness, Lloyd and Amiss, and three all-rounders (d'Oliveira, Greig and Illingworth) in their side in the early 'seventies, there were not too many vacancies for middle-order batsmen, and it was probably just as well. It was indicative of the lack of depth in this department that when they needed reinforcement on the 1974–5 tour of Australia they sent for COLIN COWDREY who was then approaching his forty-second birthday. It was his sixth trip down under, twenty years after his first, and although he had obviously been a great player he did not figure too much in the two I was on. He did not play in all the Test matches in 1970–1, although I think that was partly for political reasons. Illingworth, the dour Yorkshireman, had been preferred to Cowdrey as captain, but he had been given another Kentishman – or should it be man of Kent? – as manager in David Clark and it was not exactly a meeting of minds. At least Colin had his Kent colleague, Denness, as captain in 1974–5 and he not only went straight into the side but was asked to open the batting against Lillee and Thomson. He took a real battering, but it said everything about the quality of the man that he was prepared to face those two at their fastest with so little preparation.

He was not the only one to suffer on that tour. KEITH FLETCHER had looked a very good middle-order batsman until he came across Lillee and Thomson and then all of a sudden he was considered to be a bit of a bunny. It was not altogether fair. He was a gutsy little player and a lot tougher than he looked. He had made substantial scores against all the other countries and when his tormentors were missing from the final Test at Melbourne he and Denness really filled their boots.

JOHN HAMPSHIRE does not need reminding about Lillee, either. He had become the only Englishman to score a debut century at Lord's when he first appeared against the West Indies in 1969, but went on to play in only seven more Test matches, two of them on the 1970–1 Australian tour. He got 55 at Adelaide – I am not sure how. Lillee was making his debut and I recall him beating 'Hamps' about ten times in two (eight-ball) overs. He never looked particularly at ease after that although he still played an important part in the success of that tour. He was a terrific team man and, with his fellow Yorkshireman Don Wilson, did a great job in keeping everybody relaxed in a dressing room which contained some fairly substantial egos.

Perhaps the only England batsman who was not fazed by Lillee and Thomson, or the West Indian fast bowlers, come to that, during this period was DAVID STEELE who so captured the public imagination when he was plucked from county cricket to take them on in 1975. It was an amazing sight to see 'Steeley', with his grey hair and steel-rimmed glasses, thrusting his big front pad down the pitch against the quickest bowlers in the world. He finished at the top of the England averages that first summer, made a hundred against the West Indies the following year and was desperately unlucky not to be picked for the 1976–7 tour of India because the selectors, in their wisdom, thought that he would struggle against the spinners. Still, there was some consolation. His Test debut coincided with his benefit year and his local butcher was giving him a lamb chop for every run up to fifty and a steak and a chop for every run after that. 'Steeley' was able to stock several freezers.

✳    ✳    ●    ✳    ✳

1970–95

1   David Gower

2   Robin Smith

3   Graham Thorpe

4   Allan Lamb

5   Derek Randall

6   Mike Gatting

## All-time

1    Walter Hammond

2    Dennis Compton

3    Ken Barrington

4    Peter May

5    David Gower

6    Ted Dexter

England have had such a galaxy of middle-order batsmen over the years that DAVID GOWER is the only player from my generation who can find a place in the all-time list. WALTER HAMMOND, DENIS COMPTON and KEN BARRINGTON all averaged over 50 in Test cricket, PETER MAY was reckoned to be England's finest post-war batsman while TED DEXTER just squeezes out other great players like Sir Colin Cowdrey, Tom Graveney and Frank Woolley.

## Rest of the World

1990–5

1    Brian Lara

2    Allan Border

3    Mark Waugh

4    Mohammad Azharuddin

5    Viv Richards

6    Javed Miandad

BRIAN LARA is not simply the best batsman in the world today. He is also the best-looking, the most aesthetically pleasing, player I have seen since the great Barry Richards was in his prime. Nearly all the great batsmen have been basically orthodox players but few of them have made the game look quite as straightforward as he does. He has a lovely, relaxed stance (none of that waving the bat in the air in a manner which has seen only Graham Gooch make any real headway) and a minimum of movement at the crease. Everything else seems to follow quite naturally from that – the compact defence, the flowing strokes and the incredible string of records (375 for the West Indies against England, 501 not out for Warwickshire against Durham, etc., etc.) in 1994. What struck me particularly about his record-breaking Test innings in Antigua was his great skill at missing the fielders. No matter how defensive the field-placings became, he just kept stroking the ball along the ground and still managed to find the gaps.

Lara is a quite extraordinary talent although I have still to be convinced that he is as great a player as VIV RICHARDS, who would be my number one of all time if it were not for all that I have heard and read about Sir Donald Bradman. Viv was approaching the end of his career by the 'nineties, which is why he appears no higher than fifth on this list, but for years before that he was undoubtedly the most feared batsman in the world. I took my own fair degree of stick from the Master Blaster and I can assure you from painful experience that he really did destroy bowlers. There were so many remarkable innings but one in particular sticks in my memory. It was at The Oval in 1976 when he made 291, and I am still convinced that I had him plumb lbw when he had got about 30. Dear old Dickie Bird did not agree and Viv went on to give one of his most masterly exhibitions. You sometimes hear about batsmen 'playing by numbers'. Well, Viv sometimes seemed to be playing by numbers all right, but it was only because he had such utter contempt for the bowling. He oozed confidence, letting you know who was the boss from the moment he swaggered out of the pavilion and made his stately progress out to the middle. Once he got there, he had an amazing knack of hitting good balls for four or six – as he did with great regularity in Antigua in 1986 when he blitzed a hundred off fifty-six deliveries, the fastest in Test match history in terms of balls received. Quickness of eye was the key to it all, I think, but he had a lot more going for him besides that. Unlike Lara, he was an immensely strong man with huge forearms and biceps. He was also a member of the heavy-bat brigade and when he used all that power to hit the ball, it sure stayed hit.

Strength of a different kind is what characterised the performances of ALLAN BORDER and explains why I rate him so highly. If ever a man took the world on his shoulders, it was 'AB' when he took over as captain of a very poor Australian side in the mid-'eighties. It is easy to underestimate the problems of playing in a poor team, let alone captaining one, yet despite the lambasting he sometimes got from the media Border never let them affect his own game. A Test average of 50-plus is the hallmark of a great batsman and he not only achieved that but he did it against the toughest of opposition under the fiercest of pressure. Some of the players we are talking about did not face the West Indian fast bowlers as often as he did – and the West Indian players did not have to face them at all – but he stood up to them all and, by his own example, put some guts and character into his side. He had some classic shots against anything remotely short, either square of the wicket on the offside or off his hip down to fine leg or just behind square. He was also a terrific player of the spinners. Left-handers, remember, often have to contend with a lot of rough outside off stump and Border was a master craftsman in that respect.

In contrast to the bristling Border, MARK WAUGH always

looks very relaxed, but he has certainly made his presence felt on the cricket grounds of the world in recent times. He can sometimes seem too relaxed in that he has an infuriating habit of getting out when he is apparently well set, yet he is a superbly talented batsman and his success against the West Indies proves how good he is. It took him quite a long time to develop, his twin brother, Steve, who will feature in our all-rounders' section, getting into the Australian side five years before he did. Once he was given his chance – ironically at the expense of Steve against England at Adelaide in 1990–1 – he seized it with a classical century and he has been virtually an automatic choice ever since.

What makes cricket such a fascinating game is that we can contrast the sheer butchery of a Viv Richards with the grace of a Mark Waugh or, better still, the wristy elegance of a MOHAMMAD AZHARUDDIN. He is not physically strong at all yet he can dispatch the ball just as effectively as the most powerful players with his exquisite timing. England saw him for the first time on David Gower's tour of India in 1984–5 when he scored a century in each of his first three Tests and he has gone on to emulate Allan Border by maintaining his own personal output despite the cares of captaining a poor side.

The prodigious Sachin Tendulkar, who made such an impact when he made his first Test century against England at Old Trafford in 1990 when he was still only seventeen, is a player of similar gifts but my final choice in this period has to be JAVED MIANDAD, one of the most thoroughly annoying guys I ever played against but a mighty fine player all the same. He would have got far more recognition if he had been playing for a country other than Pakistan, whose sides have been so frequently torn apart by the political in-fighting and constant changes in captains and personnel. Javed could not complain too much about that since he was often in the thick of it and it has to be said that he did not seem to let it affect his game. He was an immensely talented player who used to amass big scores, and pretty quickly, too, when he was in the mood. He was slightly vulnerable early in his innings (who isn't?) although once he got in he usually made a lot of runs. He had to accept his fair share of flak from the quicker bowlers, and he was never afraid to take them on. He was particularly adept against the spinners, using his fleetness of foot to get down the pitch and hit them over the top.

Perhaps the most notable omission from this list is David Boon who had scored more runs for Australia than anyone apart from Allan Border when he announced his retirement from Test cricket in 1996. They called him 'The Keg on Legs' because of a capacity for beer which enabled him to break Rodney Marsh's drinking record on a flight between Sydney and London. I was more impressed with the guts he showed as a batsman, whether it was as an opener in the 'eighties or as one of the most reliable middle-order men of recent years. Unlike some players, particularly the younger brigade, he would not try to hit his way out of trouble when he was in bad nick. Instead he would simply attempt to occupy the crease and play his way out of the rut. He did it against England in 1994–5 when he was never in great form throughout the series yet spent hours at the crease waiting for his touch to come back. As it happened, it did not work for him that time but there were plenty of other occasions when it did – and against some of the fastest bowling the world has seen.

Also missing is Richie Richardson, who looked a fine player when he broke into Test cricket in the 'eighties. Ten years on, however, he seemed to have gone to pieces. He had been so badly affected by the pressures of captaining the West Indies that he had to take a break from the game because of mental fatigue and I was surprised that he was reappointed after Courtney Walsh had done an excellent job as his stand-in.

*     *     ●     *     *

1980–9

1    Viv Richards

2    Allan Border

3    Javed Miandad

4    Martin Crowe

5    Clive Lloyd

6    Alvin Kallicharran

The top three were at their best in this period but their supremacy was seriously challenged by the emergence of MARTIN CROWE as the best batsman New Zealand have ever had. He was still playing in the 'nineties but by then he was severely handicapped by a long-term knee injury and was only a shadow of the player who at his peak had been a real class act. Similar to Greg Chappell in technique, he had a lovely relaxed stance and a high back-lift and you could see how straight his bat came down when you were bowling against him. This made him a great straight-driver, as we saw when he made a century against my England side at Wellington in 1983–4 and I am sure he would have had an even more impressive Test record if he had been playing for a stronger team. Once Sir Richard Hadlee and John Wright had retired, he was left high and dry with some very mediocre players around him.

You could not say that about CLIVE LLOYD, who by the 'eighties had turned the West Indies into the most powerful side in the world, not just through his revolutionary methods as captain (and more about them later) but also through the might of his batting. Hubert was an immensely strong man with a bat as heavy as a railway sleeper. It had three and sometimes more rubber grips around the handle and he used it to great effect, whether it was in Test matches or one-day cricket. My first taste of his awesome power came when Warwickshire played Lancashire in the 1972 Gillette Cup Final and he hit me out of the ground on more than one occasion. He was always a shaky starter and early in his career the England bowlers had success in tempting him into some indiscreet hooking. Once he got in, though, he was merciless, especially with those massive straight drives of his.

Another left-hander, from a rather different mould, was ALVIN KALLICHARRAN, who I got to know very well during our time together with Warwickshire. The batsmen around him in the West Indies side – the likes of Richards, Lloyd and Rohan Kanhai – were much more powerful, but when it came to touch-play there were few better than Kallicharran. I certainly rated him a lot higher than Pakistan's Zaheer Abbas who made some huge scores – 274 not out and 240 against England among them – around the same time. I cannot put Zaheer in the top rank because while he was a very stylish player he had a distinct problem against the quicks, and on a wicket with anything in it I always fancied getting him out. Not so with Kalli. Because he was so short in stature, he was on to the short ball very quickly and never got into too much trouble against it.

1970–9

1    Viv Richards

2    Greg Chappell

3    Clive Lloyd

4    Ian Chappell

5    Rohan Kanhai

6    Doug Walters

If I had a favourite adversary during my years in Test match cricket it was IAN CHAPPELL. I first came across Ian on the 1970–1 tour of Australia. He took over the captaincy from Bill Lawry in the seventh Test of that series and I came to respect him not just because he was a particularly good player but also because he had a particularly good attitude to the game. I think his eyes had been opened a year earlier when he was part of the Australian side which was whitewashed 4–0 in South Africa in the last series before the republic was isolated from international cricket. The story goes that Ian, not sure whether 'Tiger' Lance had caught him at cover point before the ball hit the ground, turned to the fielder and asked: 'Did you catch it, Tiger?' When Lance said he had, Chappell walked off the field. Back in the dressing room, his team-mates insisted that the ball had in fact bounced, so at the next interval Chappell went up to Lance and asked him whether it had bounced or not.

'Oh, yeah,' said Lance. 'You asked me if I caught it . . . you didn't ask me if it bounced first.'

From then on, Ian played his cricket really hard but always fair. I will go into his merits as a captain later. As a batsman, he had an excellent back-foot technique against the quick bowlers although he was quite a risky hooker at times. He would always give it a go but he was much better when the ball was going safely in front of square rather than out of control down to fine leg. He was also a tremendous player of spin, with the sweep shot one of his specialities. He had many a scuffle with Derek Underwood and company and also enjoyed himself against the Indians, whom he played extremely well. He has since become an excellent albeit controversial commentator and writer and, with Geoff Boycott, is one of the two best analysts of a batsman's technique.

GREG CHAPPELL followed his elder brother into the Australian side during the 1970–1 series and when he introduced himself with a century on his debut at Perth it was evident that he was a player with a very special talent. He was a better-looking batsman than Ian, beautifully balanced at the crease, particularly on the back foot, with some memorable strokes straight down the wicket on both the off and on sides, against all types of bowling. His only real problems came in the early 'eighties when he kept getting out to the short ball against both England and the West Indies. It was something that most batsmen experience at some stage of their careers. The very good players, like Greg, get through the nightmare and make runs on the other side; the weaker brethren fall by the wayside.

My other two choices were both approaching the end of their careers in the 'seventies but they were still incredibly gifted players. ROHAN KANHAI reminded us of that in 1973 when he was one of three centurions in a massive West Indian total of 652 for 8 at Lord's which signalled the end of Raymond Illingworth's reign as captain. Rohan had quite a fiery temperament – as those of us who shared the Warwickshire dressing room with him will testify – and there was great rivalry between the top West Indian batsmen in those days when they often seemed to be trying to outdo one another. No one who saw Kanhai play will forget the way he used to fall over playing his own particular brand of legside shots. The blow I will always remember went on that legside. It came in the last over of a Benson & Hedges Cup qualifying match at Chesterfield when Mike Hendrick bowled him a low full toss and Kanhai hit it over midwicket for six – a quite extraordinary stroke.

DOUG WALTERS never did himself justice in England because he always struggled when the ball was seaming or swinging but if he got in on the good tracks in Australia it was virtually impossible to bowl at him. At home he was a devastating onside player, quite happy to hit across the line because he knew the ball was not going to deviate, and capable of accelerating at an astonishing rate. He, too, was past his best by now but he still managed to score one memorable century against us at Perth in 1974–5. He did it in a single session between tea and stumps, hitting yours truly over the distant dressing rooms to go from 97 to 103. A thoroughly nice guy, Dougie, and a very relaxed character who did not go in for the physical jerks which players indulge in nowadays. He preferred his fags and a game of cards.

\* \* ● \* \*

1970–95

1   Viv Richards

2   Brian Lara

3   Greg Chappell

4   Allan Border

5   Javed Miandad

6   Clive Lloyd

All-time

1   Sir Donald Bradman

2   Viv Richards

3   Brian Lara

4   Graeme Pollock

5   George Headley

6   Everton Weekes

With such a galaxy of talent to choose from, I am bound to ruffle a few feathers in selecting my six best middle-order batsmen of all time, although I am sure no one will argue that SIR DONALD BRADMAN with his phenomenal Test average of 99.94 must be the number one. I find it hard to believe that there have been any other better players than VIV RICHARDS and BRIAN LARA, but I have to go further back for the remaining three – GRAEME POLLOCK, the supremely gifted South African left-hander, GEORGE HEADLEY, the first of the great West Indian batsmen, who was known as 'The Black Bradman', and EVERTON WEEKES, the most charismatic of the immortal 'Three Ws'.

# 3

# NIGHTWATCHMEN

## England

1970–95

1   Alan Knott

2   Derek Underwood

3   Jack Russell

4   Eddie Hemmings

5   John Lever

6   Pat Pocock

Nightwatchmen are sent in towards the end of a day's play to protect more recognised batsmen, but two of England's best, KNOTT and RUSSELL, were good players in their own right. The beauty of using them was that if they did survive until the close they were quite capable of going out again next morning and making decent scores. Knott averaged 32 in his Test career and, judging from the way he played against South Africa in 1995–6, Russell will finish up with an average nearer 30 than 20.

Others are chosen not so much for their batting ability as for their guts and there have been no braver performances for England than those turned in by UNDERWOOD and POCOCK against the West Indian fast bowlers. 'Deadly' was once struck on the head by the fearsome Charlie Griffith but went back for more, and I can still picture him leaping like a startled rabbit with his feet off the ground and his neck snapped back trying to avoid the thunderbolts.

Pocock was at his most determined at The Oval in 1984 when he took a peppering from Holding, Marshall and Garner. He was in for forty-six minutes without actually troubling the scorers but it was a great effort.

LEVER could be a hard man to dislodge, but perhaps the most notable performance came from HEMMINGS who went in as nightwatchman against Australia at Sydney in 1982–3 and stayed to make 95.

# 4

# FAST BOWLERS

## England

1990–5

1    Devon Malcolm

2    Darren Gough

3    Martin McCague

My definition of a genuine fast bowler is someone with the ability to bowl quickly enough to unnerve batsmen with their pace, so there are not an awful lot to choose from as far as England are concerned. Many have been called to open the bowling in recent times but few have been fast enough to be included in this category which is why my 'six of the best' is confined to three who are doing their best.

DEVON MALCOLM is obviously the quickest of them. Indeed he is capable of bowling as fast as anybody in the world at the moment and I cannot help but think that England should have made more of his potential. He can produce truly devastating spells as he showed at the Foster's Oval in 1994 when he took 9 for 57 and reduced South Africa to nervous wrecks. He has also made important contributions on successive tours to the West Indies and in Australia where he would have done even better if England could have held their catches. The trouble is that he is also very wayward, with the result that both his strike rate and the runs he concedes per wicket are well out of control. An England team which is finding it so difficult to score runs themselves cannot really afford the luxury of a fast bowler whose wickets are costing getting on for forty runs apiece and who often goes for five or six an over. Devon has quite a well-controlled approach to the stumps but his problems start when he gets into his delivery stride and splays his legs wide of the crease. It is then that the radar goes adrift. Sometimes he gets it right and is almost unplayable, but more often than not he hurls the ball down the legside or pitches it short and wide of the off stump. With attacking fields, the batsman only has to get his bat on the ball and it just flies away for four. The England management seemed to have given up hope of rectifying this problem at the start of the 1995–6 tour of South Africa when Peter Lever, who had been recruited as the specialist fast bowling coach, virtually washed his hands of Devon with the words: 'He has just one asset – pace. That apart, he is a nonentity in cricketing terms.' This brought a furious reaction from Malcolm's former Derbyshire captain, Kim Barnett, and I could quite understand it. The vintage years for a fast bowler should be between the ages of twenty-eight and thirty-two and to try to tell Devon that he should be doing something different at thirty-two seemed very strange. Apart from the fact that it does not make much sense trying to change a bowler's technique once a tour is under way, I think Devon knows in his heart of hearts that he would not be able to get the ball down to the other end at anything like the same pace if he altered his action. In any case, the South African batting line-up was virtually the same as the one which Devon had blown away at The Oval. Undermining the confidence of a potentially lethal weapon was playing into South Africa's hands.

There was great excitement in English cricket when DARREN GOUGH arrived on the Test match scene with quite a flourish in 1994. He took wickets against both New Zealand and South Africa that summer and had picked up twenty in three Tests in Australia when a stress fracture of the foot stopped him in his tracks. He has not been able to recapture the original sparkle since then, coming down to earth with a bump against the West Indies in 1995 and suffering more injury problems in South Africa. There is something there, though, and I just hope that Raymond Illingworth, having plucked him out of the Yorkshire side and pitched him into international cricket, can bring it out of him. To me, Darren always seems to be straining at the leash but he is capable of bowling some very quick deliveries. He uses plenty of variety – bouncers, yorkers, off breaks, leg breaks – and he has had a lot of success with his variations of pace. What he lacks is the stock delivery. A fast bowler cannot expect to deliver six 'effort balls' every over.

MARTIN McCAGUE briefly looked the part as an England fast bowler when he made his first appearance against Australia at Trent Bridge in 1993, but quality batsmen like David Boon and Mark Waugh soon got the measure of him and I cannot remember him causing too many problems since then. He is a very strong, well-built guy with a reasonable action and he is quite a handful when he is bowling in county cricket for Kent, but he has no great control of line and length and bowls far too many half volleys and long hops to succeed at the higher level. In fact he bowled one of the worst spells ever seen in a Test match at the start of the 1994–5 tour of Australia in Brisbane, conceding twenty-six runs in his first four overs.

\* \* ● \* \*

## 1980–9

1   Bob Willis

2   Graham Dilley

3   Norman Cowans

4   Greg Thomas

England were a little bit better off for fast bowlers during this period even though I say so myself. A bloke called Willis was still around, taking his haul of wickets to 325 in Test matches, which was not a bad effort for someone with wonky knees.

We also had GRAHAM DILLEY who had a pretty good record for England (138 wickets in 41 Tests at 29.76) and should clearly have played more often than he did. He never gave the impression that he was enjoying his work but he was capable of bowling very quickly indeed and getting some beautiful, natural movement away from the right-handers. He was probably thrown in at the deep end a little bit too early in his career when he was taken on the 1979–80 Australian tour at the age of twenty, but England are not the only country who are guilty of doing that to their young fast bowlers. As soon as they see a bowler of any real pace, the selectors want to get him into the side as soon as possible. Graham was a rare sight in modern cricket in that he had a long drag. It was fairly common in the 'fifties but it has now gone right out of fashion and you do not see many fast bowlers with steel drag plates on their toe-caps these days.

I really thought that I had a discovery on my hands when NORMAN COWANS, then only twenty-one years old, just shaded Gladstone Small for the last fast bowling berth on the 1982–3 tour of Australia. He bowled very quickly at times on that tour and certainly had the sign over the great Greg Chappell whom he dismissed for nought and two on his way to the man-of-the-match award in our remarkable three-run win at Melbourne. On returning to county cricket, however, Norman realised that life might be easier at a reduced pace and tried to turn himself into a swing bowler. His performances for England were never the same after that and he drifted away from the England scene. By the time he left Middlesex for Hampshire in 1993, he was only a shadow of the bowler he had once been. It was a shame because Norman had a classic run-up and action, and, at the start of his career, real pace – all the attributes you need to be a top-class fast bowler. Sadly it was not to be.

GREG THOMAS was another who looked like answering our prayers for a real fast bowler when we took him on the 1985–6 tour of the West Indies. Again we were in for a disappointment. He could certainly propel a cricket ball at great speed and I well remember him sitting as good a batsman as Gordon Greenidge on his backside on a fast pitch at Sabina Park. However, he had very little control and, unfortunately, very little common sense when it came to bowling fast. I was the assistant manager on that trip and I recall taking him on to the outfield at the Queen's Park Oval in Trinidad and trying to get him to bowl twelve balls in the same place. Even that simple exercise was beyond him. He wanted to experiment all the time with bouncers and yorkers but, as I said in regard to Darren Gough, it is so important for quick bowlers to have a stock delivery that they can rely on before stepping up the tempo for the faster stuff. It is one thing bowling bouncers and yorkers; it is quite another getting your line back afterwards.

I suppose I could have included Chris Old and Gladstone Small in this section because they were both capable of bowling fast at times but I think they come more into the seam and swing category.

1970–9

1    John Snow

2    Bob Willis

3    Peter Lever

4    Alan Ward

5    John Price

6    Ken Shuttleworth

JOHN SNOW was, without a doubt, England's best fast bowler since the Trueman–Statham era and it was little short of a scandal that he played in no more than forty-nine Test matches. He rarely saw eye to eye with the selectors or even his captains and was obviously left out of several tours, including the 1974–5 trip to Australia, for disciplinary reasons after knocking over India's Sunil Gavaskar when he was going for a sharp single at Lord's in 1971. That was England's loss because Snowy was a quite brilliant bowler with a lovely, relaxed approach to the wicket and a seemingly effortless delivery stride. His critics did not think so but he worked very hard at his bowling in his own way. He was very much a rhythm bowler and he believed he knew what was best for him. He was absolutely superb on Ray Illingworth's Ashes-winning tour in 1970–1 even though his 'throat ball' length sometimes incurred the wrath of the Australian umpires as their batsmen struggled to play him. He also had success in the West Indies, and in trying to assess any fast bowler, whether he is from England or elsewhere, I think it is worth examining their records in the Caribbean. To get wickets there, you need to be a fast bowler of remarkable talent. Suffice it to say that John Snow took twenty-seven in four Test matches on the 1967–8 tour.

No one can say that PETER LEVER, England's current fast

bowling coach, does not know his subject, since he could be genuinely quick himself, certainly down-wind with a good head of steam to fire him up. He did not have the classical action of a Trueman or a Snow but he had a good approach to the wicket which proved effective for him as he took the ball naturally away from the right-handers. He sprang to prominence by bowling out the powerful Rest of the World side in their last representative match against England at The Oval in 1970 and went on to become an important support bowler on both the 1970–1 and 1974–5 tours of Australia. He was never quite the same after he struck New Zealand's Ewan Chatfield on the head and only the kiss of life from England's physiotherapist, Bernard Thomas, saved Chatfield's life.

ALAN WARD and KEN SHUTTLEWORTH, who both went on the 1970–1 trip to Australia, did not achieve as much as they might have done because of injuries and it was their misfortune which gave me my first chance in Test match cricket. Ward was a seriously quick bowler who had terrified the 1969 New Zealanders and was expected to do the same to the Australians, but he was injured before the Test series even started and had to return home. I was flown out as his replacement and found myself playing in the fourth Test at Sydney when 'Shut' also broke down. He finished up playing in only five Test matches (the same as Ward), which was a pity because he was a fine sight in full flow with his Trueman-like action and the ability to hit the deck very hard.

Talking of fine sights, there were few more amazing actions than that of JOHN PRICE with his long, curving run-up and enormous drag which enabled him to generate a lot of pace. He was another bowler who suffered a lot from injuries but he certainly made the batsmen hop about a bit in the late 'sixties and early 'seventies, especially the Indians. Gavaskar, who played against all the great fast bowlers of the day, reckons that 'Sport' Price produced one of the quickest spells he ever faced.

1970–95

1    John Snow

2    Bob Willis

3    Graham Dilley

4    Peter Lever

5    Devon Malcolm

6    Darren Gough

All-time

1    Fred Trueman

2    Harold Larwood

3    John Snow

4    Bob Willis

5    Brian Statham

6    Frank Tyson

Go on, then, argue about it among yourselves.

## Rest of the World

1990–5

1     Courtney Walsh

2     Curtly Ambrose

3     Waqar Younis

4     Craig McDermott

5     Allan Donald

6     Malcolm Marshall

The rest of the world has certainly been blessed with a few more fast bowlers than dear old England have in recent years, which is as good a reason as any why we have not been all that successful at Test match level.

None of them has been more formidable than the West Indian spearhead, CURTLY AMBROSE, the 6ft 7in Antiguan, who bowls the ball straight up your nose. He went off the boil a bit in the mid-'nineties because of an aggravating shoulder injury but at his peak he was a devastating bowler with superb control of length. He has a bouncy, business-like run-up and a superb high action from which he can bring the ball down on a sixpence time after time. His extra height enables him to get the ball to rear off a good length, and on pitches of uneven bounce which we have seen in the Caribbean lately he is unplayable. He does not overuse the bouncer for the simple reason that he does not need to – batsmen, tail-enders in particular, have been known to take evasive action against his length ball! – and he has that very special knack of producing telling spells just when they are needed most. He did it against England in Barbados in 1989–90 (8 for 45) and Trinidad in 1993–4 (6 for 24); against South Africa in Barbados in 1991–2 (6 for 34); and against

*Top:* Two of the greatest opening batsmen of my time – Sunil Gavaskar and Geoff Boycott.

*Bottom:* Michael Slater exudes the joy of batting while Gordon Greenidge and Desmond Haynes take a break in the middle of another partnership.

*Top:* Allan Border (left) became Australia's top run-maker but Graham Thorpe has still to turn those fifties into hundreds.

*Bottom:* Robin Smith, one of the few batsmen who actually relishes the short stuff.

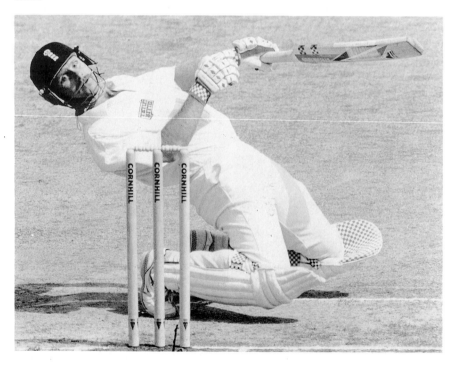

*Top:* Sir Donald Bradman, the greatest the world has seen, together with a youthful David Gower, one of the finest middle-order batsmen ever produced by England.

*Bottom:* Two phenomenal West Indians – Brian Lara (left) and Viv Richards.

Courtney Walsh – my number one fast bowler of the early 'nineties.

*Top:* Allan Donald (left), a model for any fast bowler, and Devon Malcolm, who does not have quite the same degree of accuracy.

*Bottom:* The pride of Pakistan – Waqar Younis (left) and Wasim Akram after their triumph in England in 1992.

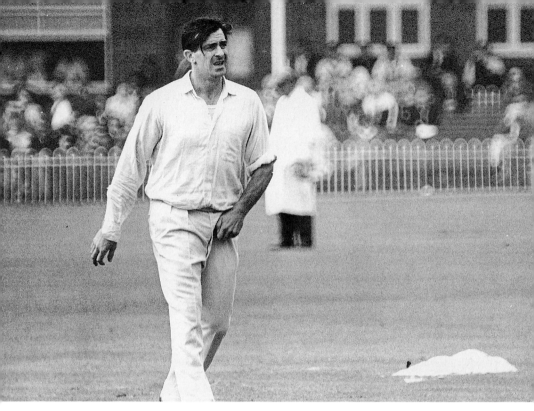

Fred Trueman (top), England's finest fast bowler, and John Snow, the best we have had since.

Dennis Lillee in 1974–5 – we knew we were watching a very rare talent.

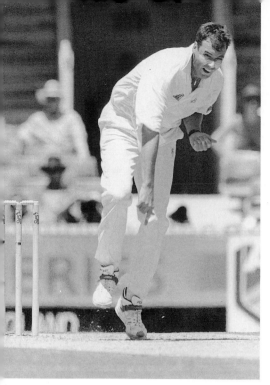

*Top:* Angus Fraser (left) was a captain's dream but even Dickie Bird had to tell Kenny Benjamin to pitch it up.

*Bottom:* Chris Old, the best seam bowler of my generation.

Australia at Perth in 1992–3 (7 for 1 in 32 balls). And they are just the performances which spring immediately to mind.

In view of the devastation Ambrose can cause, you may find it strange that I have not put him at the top of my list, but I do believe that COURTNEY WALSH has been the most effective and, when he steps up a gear, the most intimidating bowler of the 'nineties. He has never had the plaudits of his contemporaries and at one time he was such an underestimated member of the West Indian attack that he was not even sure of his place in the side, but he has removed whatever doubts they had about him with his sheer consistency. Whether he is playing for the West Indies, his native Jamaica or his adopted county, Gloucestershire, whether he is operating on the uneven pitches of the Caribbean or the flat tracks of India, he never seems to wilt under pressure but just keeps charging in to bowl, over after over, day after day. He has got himself extremely fit and rarely seems to suffer from the kind of injuries which afflict most fast bowlers. He has a lithe run-up to the wicket and puts enormous effort into his delivery stride. And his stamina is quite amazing. I remember him bowling a spell of fourteen overs during the Jamaica Test against England in 1992–3, in which he gave Michael Atherton a real peppering, and still having the strength to come back and bombard Devon Malcolm at the end of the innings. He is a quite brilliant exponent of the yorker and, even in his longest spells, he can bowl the most vicious bouncers. One or two eyebrows have been raised about his action, especially when he bowls his 'quicker' ball, but for my money his arm is perfectly straight whether he is bowling yorkers, bouncers or good-length balls.

Unlike Ambrose and Walsh, MALCOLM MARSHALL was not a tall man but, right up until his retirement at the end of the 1991 England tour, he was perhaps the most complete of all the West Indian fast bowlers. He had a very active, bouncy run-up and exploded like a coiled spring to deliver the ball at extreme pace. It could skid on to the batsman at an alarming rate off the most bland of surfaces, as I can testify, having been hit on the wrist just in front of my rather large nose when I was taking evasive action against him at Lord's in 1984. Marshall had brilliant control, very rarely skewing the ball down the legside, and his ability to swing it at high speed made him the West Indies' record wicket-taker with 376 victims. His most remarkable performance in England was at Headingley in 1984 when he was told not to play cricket for at least ten days after suffering a double fracture of the left thumb while fielding in the gully on the first morning. Not only did he defy doctor's orders by batting left-handed to enable Larry Gomes to complete a century but he then blew England away with his best Test figures of 7 for 53. More than any of the West Indians, perhaps, Marshall benefited from his experience in county cricket with Hampshire. In return, he always gave of his best for them and it was a shame for him that they did not have more success while he was there. They certainly should have done.

English cricket has also been good to ALLAN DONALD whose experience with Warwickshire had made him just about the finished article by the time South Africa made their long-awaited return to Test cricket and he was soon enjoying the success which we all thought would come his way at international level. He had a huge responsibility with South Africa's only other genuinely quick bowler, Brett Schultz, having a lot of injury problems and he has shouldered it well with staunch support from the likes of Chris Matthews, Fanie De Villiers, Brian McMillan and, more recently, the emerging Shaun Pollock. Donald has a classical style, a straight, busy but very controlled run-up followed by a slight delay and then a leap in the air, a high front arm and a beautiful side-on action with a brilliant follow-through. It is faultless and if it was possible to teach somebody the art of bowling fast he would be the perfect model. We saw him at his best in England in 1995 when he was determined to be as great an influence on the Warwickshire side as Brian Lara had been the year before and he did it superbly. For the most part, Dermot Reeve bowled him in short spells but occasionally he had to bowl for longer periods and he responded magnificently to the extra workload. Not all overseas fast bowlers – not all English fast bowlers, come to that – have always been able to give of their best at county level but there has never been any question mark against Allan Donald in that respect. Of all the spells I have seen him bowl, only the one against Graham Gooch and Michael Atherton at the end of the 1994 series in England has been wild and reckless. The rest of the time his control has been absolutely superb for a bowler of such extreme pace.

Much the same goes for CRAIG McDERMOTT, who, when he is fit, is a fast bowler of the highest class and a real handful for the world's best batsmen. And we saw on England's tour of Australia in 1994–5 what a great competitor he is. Some Press criticism, probably to do with his fitness record, had obviously got to him and he went out determined to prove a point, which he did by bowling with great stamina and great skill as well. The Australians had clearly done their homework on the England batsmen and McDermott followed the script perfectly. He was only nineteen when he made his Test debut against the West Indies in 1984–5 and in those early days he could only really bowl on wickets with a bit of pace and bounce to help him but as he has matured and developed he has been able to get good batsmen out on any surface. He can bowl from very close to the stumps, which is quite unusual for a big man, and he maintains a very searching line, which means that a batsman who is looking to leave the ball as much as possible early in his innings is not at liberty to do so. He can also make the new ball bounce towards the left nipple, which apart from being a very difficult area for the batsman to defend is also a very painful place to get hit, and he has picked up quite a few wickets as they fend it off to the wicketkeeper, short leg or a well-positioned leg slip.

McDermott would be the first to pay tribute to the support he has received over the years from Merv Hughes whose guts and determination played a major part in Australia's climb to ascendancy in the Test match arena. As one of only three seam bowlers, he bowled more than his share of overs, often into the wind, and did a great job for both Allan Border and Mark Taylor. He always seemed to take a particular delight in bowling at Graeme Hick, giving him a really testing time with deliveries aimed at the body.

Like Hughes, Ian Bishop does not figure in my 'six of the best' but I would like to pay my own tribute to him for the way he has fought back from some devastating back injuries which threatened his career just when he had established himself as one of the best fast bowlers in the world. Fitness and strength have been the keys to the West Indies' success and there has been no better example of the hard work this requires than Bishop's long struggle to get back into Test cricket. It meant endless months of recuperation, countless hours in the gym and then the challenge of proving his fitness with Trinidad in the hard school of Red Stripe Cup cricket. It also meant remodelling his action, and how well he has done it. He is now so open-chested that one would expect he would only be able to bowl inswingers but this was not the case at all on the 1995 England tour when he proved to be an inspired selection. He still had the ability to make the ball move away from the right-handers at high speed and he was not afraid to dig it in short, either. I think the West Indians, as a group, bowled too short on that tour and would have had much greater success if they had listened to Michael Holding pleading with them to pitch the ball up. That takes nothing away from Bishop's remarkable recovery. Some of his spells were fairly innocuous, while others were quite breathtaking and I think there may be more to come from him yet.

Talking of injuries, it is going to be fascinating to see whether WAQAR YOUNIS can recover from the severe back problem which forced him to cry off county cricket with Surrey and seriously disrupted his international career with Pakistan. Waqar has quite a long run-up and a whippy action which has clearly put too much stress on his back and he was a sorry sight when he began his comeback against Sri Lanka in 1995. Before that, however, he was a fantastic fast bowler, a new phenomenon really in that he pitched it up most of the time and used reverse swing to bowl quite unplayable yorkers with the old ball. If anything is going to mop up tail-enders it is a ball bowled at nearly a hundred miles per hour straight at their big toe with a little bit of late inswing to rearrange the furniture. To me, as a child of the 'sixties, a fast bowler actually preferring a battered old ball to a shiny new one is absolute heresy but times have obviously changed. It all came about because of the unresponsive pitches on the subcontinent, and, by fair means or foul, the old ball has certainly moved around for the great exponents of reverse swing. Imran Khan had a huge influence on the development of Waqar and his equally destructive partner, Wasim Akram, and they enabled him to transform the fortunes of Pakistan. It was not until their arrival that Pakistan managed to put together the kind of results they should have been getting much earlier in their history.

1980–9

1    Malcolm Marshall

2    Michael Holding

3    Joel Garner

4    Dennis Lillee

5    Andy Roberts

6    Jeff Thomson

I think it was the emergence of ANDY ROBERTS as a top-class fast bowler which put the West Indies on their way to becoming the dominant force in world cricket. We had our first good look at him when he forced his way into their Test side on the 1973-4 tour of the Caribbean and he rapidly matured into a devastating quick bowler. He may not have been as aesthetically pleasing as the likes of Wes Hall and Michael Holding, with his angled run-up, relatively low action and long bowling arm and delivery stride, but the end product was just as effective. He was totally undemonstrative on the field and just went about his business of being an assassin with a cricket ball with mechanical skill and cool, calculated aggression. Behind that unsmiling countenance was a very friendly guy and if you did manage to get a few words out of him they were usually worth listening to. His intelligence both as a man and as a bowler shone through every time he had a cricket ball in his hands and it is no wonder that the other West Indian fast bowlers revered him.

One of his disciples was MICHAEL HOLDING, another intelligent man who was a real student of fast bowling and indeed the game in general. He also made his first appearance in 1973-4, playing for the President's XI in our first match in Barbados, and I remember him pulling up after a few overs with a damaged hamstring. He soon got himself fit again, however, and it was not long before his beautiful action was a familiar sight around the world. The English umpires nicknamed him 'Whispering Death' because they could not hear him approaching on his wonderfully smooth, light-footed run-up, and his rhythm was so perfect that he hardly ever bowled a no-ball. Even when he was kicking over the stumps in New Zealand in an uncharacteristic outburst against the perceived bias of the umpiring it was like poetry in motion. People still talk about his extraordinary performance in the final Test at the Kennington Oval in 1976 when he took fourteen wickets on a featherbed pitch and his incredible over at the Kensington Oval in 1980-1 when he made even Geoffrey Boycott look like a novice. Holding was probably the best example of the modern fast bowler who looks more like an Olympic athlete than an old-fashioned cricketer. He always took a set of dumb-bells on tour to keep his upper torso honed to perfection and would go on long runs with Dennis Waight, the West Indies' faithful Australian physiotherapist, to build up his stamina. The message is one that I have never been able to get across to England fast bowlers. I learned the hard way that you have to get yourself physically fit to do the job.

With fast bowlers like Roberts and Holding opening the attack,

JOEL GARNER usually had to be content with coming on as first or second change and I have often wondered how much more devastating he might have been if he had been able to take the new ball. Joel looked like Gulliver among the Lilliputians as he bounded effortlessly up to the wicket and delivered the ball with a long sweep of his huge right arm, and the advantage of being 6ft 8in tall enabled him to get it to climb almost vertically from a good length. He was a little reminiscent of Vintcent Van Der Bijl, the giant South African who played for Middlesex, but Garner's extra strength made him much more of a handful. He captained the West Indies in the World Masters Series at Bombay in 1995 and he was still a force to be reckoned with. He was always an intensely fierce competitor and he was determined to win that series and carry off the £50,000 winner's cheque. It was a serious business for the West Indian over-35s.

From the moment we saw DENNIS LILLEE making his Test debut against England at Adelaide in 1970–1 until his retirement in 1983–4 with the then record of 355 wickets, we always knew that we were watching a very rare talent indeed. It took him a little while to develop his tremendous control but he was almost the finished article by the time he came to England in 1972 and took thirty-one wickets in the five Tests. The following year he suffered a horrendous back injury in the Caribbean and we did not believe he would be able to come back from it when we went to Australia again in 1974–5. How wrong we were. He had not only got himself fit again but in company with a new phenomenon called Jeff Thomson he simply terrorised our batsmen. It showed the determination of the man. He knew that fast bowlers have to expect a bit of pain and heartache and he trained himself to a standstill to build up his strength and stamina. He had a rather flat-footed run-up, but with 80,000 Aussies chanting 'Lillee, Lillee' and 'Kill, kill, kill' it was enough to fill most batsmen with dread and when he got to the crease his action was just about perfect. Good players who did not quite get into the 'great' category, players like Mike Denness, Dennis Amiss and Keith Fletcher, were easy pickings for Lillee who seemed to get them out almost before they had taken guard – and he did not need any help from the pitch to do it, either. When the wickets were flat and slow, he was quite content to bowl leg-cutters, which he did when he bowled us out with eleven wickets in the match at Melbourne in 1979–80. Three years earlier on the same ground in the Centenary Test he had bowled for long spells to pick up another eleven wickets, and although Derek Randall was named man of the match by a panel of 'experts', any right-thinking person would have given the award to D. K. Lillee. For some time, Lillee did benefit from having the extreme pace of Thomson at the other end but even when he had to bowl with lesser lights he was just as effective. A tremendous character, he is still the oldest teenager in town and it is great fun to be with him socially. It was not so enjoyable to meet him on the cricket field.

Just as we were wrong about Lillee and his ability to recover from injury, so we were wrong about JEFF THOMSON when we first heard about the new fast bowler who was causing something of a stir after being dragged off the beach in Sydney. We imagined he would be a bit like his namesake, Alan 'Froggy' Thomson, who had been supposed to scare us four years earlier and had turned out to be more hype than anything else. Tommo's slinging, javelin-style action looked strange when we saw it for the first time and occasionally he was as wild and wayward as Froggy had been, but, when you came to think about it, it was quite a natural way to deliver a cricket ball. Indeed it is strange that fast bowling coaches have not chosen to teach youngsters to bowl like he did because he was mighty effective. He was certainly capable of joining the fast bowlers' '300 club' and surely would have done but for two freak injuries to his right shoulder, one while playing tennis on the rest day of the Adelaide Test in 1974–5, the other when he crashed into Alan Turner when they went for the same catch in the first Test against Pakistan in 1976–7, again at Adelaide. He was not the same force after that and although he managed to keep going until the 1985 tour of England, he had become a pale imitation of his former self. He had seen both sides of the coin in Australian cricket – the heady days of the 'seventies and the shambolic period in the 'eighties.

1970–9

1   Dennis Lillee

2   Andy Roberts

3   Jeff Thomson

4   Michael Holding

5   Colin Croft

6   Graham McKenzie

Until the advent of Lillee and Thomson, Australia's number one fast bowler was GRAHAM McKENZIE who managed to pick up 246 Test wickets despite playing most of his cricket in the 'sixties and early 'seventies when the wickets were at their best for batting. It was somewhat ironic that he should have to take a nasty smack in the mouth from John Snow on a bad pitch at Sydney in 1970–1, although he hit a few batsmen in his time, breaking Geoff Boycott's arm and sending the West Indies' Jackie Hendriks to hospital for brain surgery. All cricket lovers of a certain age will remember his extraordinary delivery stride as he stretched out his long front leg and heaved his mighty physique through a beautiful side-on action which gave him real pace and quite vicious movement off the seam. It became almost as familiar in England as it was in Australia when he joined Leicestershire and helped Raymond Illingworth turn that supposed bunch of no-hopers into a championship-winning side.

There were plenty of other quality fast bowlers around in this period, including Pakistan's Sarfraz Nawaz, reputedly the god-father of reverse swing, Vanburn Holder, the last of the old-fashioned West Indian quicks, and Wayne Daniel and Sylvester Clarke, who were among the first of the new breed. But perhaps the meanest of them all in modern times was COLIN CROFT who was quoted as saying that he did not just want to intimidate the batsmen but he wanted to inflict physical pain as well. Croft was a very awkward customer indeed with his open-chested action and wide-of-the-crease delivery which sent the ball spearing into the right-handers and left them with no escape route. Tall and strong, he was as dangerous a bowler as any the West Indies have ever had and when he was playing with Roberts, Holding and Garner completed the most devastating quartet the game has seen.

\*     \*     ●     \*     \*

1970–95

1    Dennis Lillee

2    Malcolm Marshall

3    Andy Roberts

4    Michael Holding

5    Jeff Thomson

6    Curtly Ambrose

### All-time

As above. Cricket is full of fast bowling legends from Fred 'The Demon' Spofforth and Ray Lindwall of Australia to Wes Hall and Charlie Griffith of the West Indies but I will take some convincing that any of them were faster or better than my top six from the 1970–95 period.

# 5

## SPIN BOWLERS

England

1990–5

1    Phil Tufnell

2    Richard Illingworth

3    John Emburey

4    Eddie Hemmings

5    Peter Such

6    Ian Salisbury

English spin bowling has never been at a lower ebb than it was in the early 'nineties. It was a sad indictment of our resources when JOHN EMBUREY was recalled for the fourth Test against the West Indies at Old Trafford in 1995 just before his forty-third birthday. Not surprisingly, he did not take a wicket in his thirty overs and had little influence on England's six-wicket victory. Emburey still managed to take seventy-four wickets for Middlesex before going off to manage Northamptonshire and the England A team but that was more of a reflection of the poor standard of county cricket than anything else. PHIL TUFNELL picked up another sixty-eight wickets at the other end and the fact that the pair of them have had such great success for Middlesex year after year illustrates the glaring lack of technique in the English game against spin bowling of any quality, never mind spin bowling of world class.

The harsh reality is that the only match-winning performances we have seen at Test match level in recent times have come from Tufnell and they have been few and far between. The most spectacular came at the Foster's Oval in 1991 when he took six wickets for four runs in thirty-three balls against the West Indies, although that was not so much a case of him destroying them with his spin as them committing suicide with the bat. Tufnell went on to win two more Test matches – against Sri Lanka at Lord's (5 for 94) and against New Zealand at Christchurch (7 for 47) – but he has had only one other five-wicket haul in his entire Test career. He is a hugely talented bowler, no question, although having been his manager at under-19 level in the Caribbean, I have always doubted whether he could succeed at the highest level. My report on that trip – and I have flicked through it once or twice to remind myself – made it clear that he was always going to be a difficult player to handle, especially on tour. Sure enough, he has run into disciplinary problems with successive tour managements and although he looks more comfortable at home his fragile temperament will invariably allow a persistent batsman to get the better of him. He will always have more patience than Tuffers.

It is hard to think of a more contrasting character than the earnest John Ernest Emburey yet for all his nous and knowhow his overall Test record has been disappointing – 147 wickets in 64 Tests at nearly 38 runs apiece with only six bags of five wickets or more. He certainly looked the part with his classical high action which enabled him to get quite a bit of bounce when he took sixteen wickets in four Test matches on his first tour of Australia in 1978–9, and he has undoubtedly been the best off-spinner in England ever since. His bowling suffered, however, from the requirements of one-day cricket in which spinners are more concerned with saving runs than taking wickets. He had his moments, especially on Mike Gatting's Ashes-winning tour of Australia in 1986–7 when he took seven wickets in the Sydney Test, but by then he was more of a defensive bowler than a wicket-taker and his captains used him in that role to give the quicker men a breather.

EDDIE HEMMINGS got his first chance at the ripe old age of thirty-three in 1982 when Emburey was serving the first of his two lengthy suspensions for taking part in 'rebel' tours of South Africa, and was still in the England side in Australia nine years later. He tried to be a carbon copy of Tom Cartwright in his early days as a seamer at Edgbaston, then switched halfway through his career to bowling off-spin for Warwickshire, Nottinghamshire and finally

Sussex, where he played until he was forty-six. Eddie certainly spun the ball and enjoyed great success on the pitches Ron Allsopp created at Trent Bridge in the 'eighties, and although he distinguished himself on my tour of Australia in 1982–3 by scoring 95 not out after going in as nightwatchman at Sydney, he could not do the job he was really there to do on a turning pitch.

It looked as though PETER SUCH, once Eddie's apprentice at Nottingham, was going to have a decent career as an England off-spinner when he took 6 for 67 on a damp pitch at Old Trafford in his first Test against Australia in 1993. However, he has been unable to convince the selectors that he is worth a regular place in the side. He is not a huge spinner of the ball and very different to both Emburey and Hemmings although he is reasonably accurate and I think he has been unlucky not to be picked more often. The problem is that it is much more difficult for off-spinners to take wickets in Test cricket than it used to be. They are treated with such disdain in the one-day game that they have to prove that they are a cut above the average to be given any respect at Test level.

Wrist-spinners are a different matter and there was a roll of drums when IAN SALISBURY made his Test debut against Pakistan in 1992 and became the first leg-spinner to play for England since Robin Hobbs in the late 'sixties and early 'seventies. Unfortunately for him, he came on to the scene at the same time as Shane Warne, Anil Kumble and Mushtaq Ahmed and this has made it very tough for him. If they had not been around he may have looked a much better bowler. Comparisons are inevitable, though, and he does not present anything like the same kind of threat at international level. Ian is a very competitive cricketer and a particular favourite of Christopher Martin-Jenkins, the *Daily Telegraph* correspondent, who seems to include him in every England side he picks. He does get plenty of turn and he has a decent googly, but for me he bowls far too many bad balls to be a realistic proposition. From a romantic point of view, it would be very nice to have a leg-spinner in the England side; however, Salisbury is always going to be too expensive to be selected on a regular basis.

At the other extreme is RICHARD ILLINGWORTH, Worcestershire's Yorkshire-born left-arm spinner, who took a wicket with his first ball in Test cricket when he bowled the West Indies' Phil Simmons at Trent Bridge in 1991. He bowled the great Viv Richards as well later on, but even so, I still thought he looked very ordinary and was not surprised that his England appearances were confined to one-day cricket for a long time after that. He seemed to be much too defensive in his outlook although I have been impressed by his recent development which earned him a recall against the West Indies in 1995 and a place on the South African tour. He now has a slower, more controlled approach to the wicket and is certainly getting more turn.

*     *     ●     *     *

1980–9

1    Derek Underwood

2    Phil Edmonds

3    John Emburey

4    Pat Pocock

5    Eddie Hemmings

6    Nick Cook

Now we are talking. DEREK UNDERWOOD, otherwise known as 'Deadly', would probably have finished up as England's top wicket-taker of all time if he had not gone off to play for Kerry Packer's World Series Cricket in 1977–8 and then effectively finished his Test match career by joining the 'rebel' tour of South Africa four years later. By then, he had taken 297 Test wickets, over a hundred more than any other England spin bowler, and the mind boggles at how many he might have picked up if he had continued playing at the highest level. Deadly was quite unique in that he was almost a medium-paced spin bowler who was absolutely unplayable on wet wickets in the days when they were left uncovered. He was seen at his most devastating in the final Test against Australia at The Oval in 1968 when a thunderstorm which flooded the ground at lunchtime seemed to have robbed England of their chance of squaring the series. Spectators joined ground staff in a frantic mopping-up operation, but even then Australia still had four wickets left with only thirty-five minutes remaining. Deadly took them all in the space of twenty-seven deliveries. It was on another wet pitch that he achieved his best Test figures of 8 for 51 against Pakistan at Lord's in 1974, yet he could also bowl very well on dry dustbowls where he would vary his pace to great effect. His greatest asset was his accuracy and he would spend long periods in Test matches just blocking up one end while the seamers took it in turns to bowl down-wind at the other. He could bowl maiden after maiden and would become intensely frustrated if other bowlers were not interested in doing the same. The ability to bowl maiden overs is a very important part of any bowler's repertoire, whether they are fast or slow, and Derek just loved the challenge of keeping the best batsmen quiet. For reasons which I could never understand, Ray Illingworth sometimes preferred to have Norman Gifford in his side, but Deadly was an automatic choice for Mike Denness, Tony Greig and Mike Brearley, and I was very surprised when he signed up to play for Kerry Packer. He had always seemed to be English through and through – even to the extent of standing up on his own and refusing to contemplate strike action when the other players did not want to play a seventh Test in Australia in 1970–1.

PAT POCOCK, whose twenty-five Test matches for England spanned seventeen years between the 1967–8 tour of the West Indies and the 1984–5 trip to India, was a completely different kettle of fish. I saw quite a bit of 'Percy' both in my early days with Surrey and when we were playing together in the England side, and he always seemed to be too easily distracted from the job in hand. He was prone to experiment too much instead of following Underwood's example of bowling maidens on flat pitches and trying to frustrate the batsmen into errors. He probably had more theories about off-spin bowling than Ted Dexter had about batting, but his Test record – 67 wickets at 44 runs each – does not bear too much inspection. He should certainly have played in more Tests and taken more wickets because he was quite a big spinner of the ball. In fact he used to spin it so hard that he would get terrible lacerations on his spinning finger which he was constantly dipping in balsam to try to harden the skin.

PHIL EDMONDS, who was to succeed Underwood as England's regular left-arm spinner, was another very talented bowler who used to get bored just trying to bowl maidens and was liable to experiment at any moment. He had picked up five wickets in his first twelve overs in Test cricket against Australia at Headingley in

1975 before vandals sabotaged the pitch and caused the match to be abandoned, and although the Australians had contributed to their own downfall by getting out to some unbelievable rubbish, he looked like having a very worthwhile Test career. He was a very difficult character to handle, though, and when I was captain I eventually decided that it was better to leave him out of the side altogether rather than try to cope with his strange temperament. One example of the kind of thing that really got my goat was when he suddenly bowled a bouncer against Richard Hadlee at The Oval in 1983 and nearly decapitated our wicketkeeper, Bob Taylor. Edmonds should certainly have gone on the tours of Australia in 1982–3 and New Zealand and Pakistan in 1983–4 but, like Mike Brearley before me, I had lost patience with him by then and he did not get selected.

It was partly because of our frustration with the Edmonds temperament and partly because he had ricked his back getting out of his car, that NICK COOK was given his opportunity against New Zealand at Lord's in 1983. He could not have made a much better start, taking five wickets in the first innings and eight in the match, and another nine wickets at Trent Bridge earned him a place on the winter tour. Unfortunately we were soon to discover what an ordinary bowler he really was. We were looking to him to bowl New Zealand out in their second innings at Wellington after we had taken a first innings lead of 244 but he managed to take only three wickets in sixty-six overs.

Another spinner who did not quite make the grade was Vic Marks who had the misfortune to come across a swashbuckling tail-ender called Harry Frei in the match against Queensland at the start of the 1982–3 tour of Australia. Frei hit him for 38 in two overs and poor old Victor was not called on to take any part in the Test series. It was not an unusual experience for him since he had learned his trade at Taunton where the boundaries are very short, and with the likes of Botham and Garner bowling for Somerset the batsmen were always looking to get after him. He was a bright bloke, though, and by giving the ball plenty of air he not only picked up a lot of wickets in county cricket but played a very useful role for England in one-day matches.

1970–9

1    Derek Underwood

2    Fred Titmus

3    Ray Illingworth

4    John Emburey

5    Phil Edmonds

6    Pat Pocock

There have been few more durable cricketers than FRED TITMUS, who had been floating his off-spinners in during five decades when he finally called it a day in 1982. He had made his first-class debut for Middlesex in 1949, when he was only sixteen, and was still good enough to be recalled to the England side for his third tour of Australia and his seventh in all in 1974–5 when he was past forty. It was the sheer economy of his run-up and action which enabled him to play for so long even though he had lost four toes when he got his foot trapped in the propellers of a motor boat in the West Indies in 1967–8. He had such tremendous control of flight that he almost seemed to have the ball on a string as he took more than a hundred wickets in a season sixteen times. He was also a good enough batsman to complete the double eight times. Fred finished with 153 Test wickets, his best figures of 7 for 79 coming at Sydney in 1962–3, although he did not have such a happy time twelve years later. In fact he became utterly frustrated because the Australian umpires just would not give the batsmen out lbw when they played the sweep shot and missed. English off-spinners bowl a different line from their Australian counterparts who pitch the ball well wide of the off stump rather than bowling wicket to wicket. This is because they have always had a restriction of five players on the legside in Australia, and now that it seems likely to become

standard in world cricket I think it is going to make life very difficult for off-spinners. Fred was past his best by then, of course, but
he remained such a high-class bowler that he was still able to return
to play a part in Middlesex's championship successes of 1981 and
1982.

RAY ILLINGWORTH, who features more in both the all-
rounders' and captains' sections, was a different type of off-spinner
altogether, although on occasions he probably gave the ball even
more air than Fred did. He had been brought up on uncovered
wickets and was somewhat reminiscent of Jim Laker in his delivery
stride if not his approach to the wicket. Jack Birkenshaw suffered
a bit through playing under Illy at Leicestershire. He either had to
bowl at the less favourable end when the ball was turning or he had
to bowl more than his fair share of overs when the wickets were
flat. He was certainly not as good a bowler as Illingworth but he
did a reasonable job on his two tours, to India and Pakistan in
1972–3 and the West Indies in 1973–4.

\*      \*      ●      \*      \*

1970–95

1   Derek Underwood

2   Fred Titmus

3   Ray Illingworth

4   John Emburey

5   Phil Edmonds

6   Pat Pocock

## All-time

1   Jim Laker

2   Derek Underwood

3   Hedley Verity

4   Johnny Wardle

5   Tony Lock

6   Fred Titmus

Any spin bowler who could take nineteen wickets in a Test match against Australia has got to be the greatest so JIM LAKER tops my list. I rated DEREK UNDERWOOD highly enough to put him ahead of the two Yorkshire left armers, HEDLEY VERITY and JOHNNY WARDLE, although TONY LOCK would no doubt have had something to say about his position in the order. FRED TITMUS more than earned the final place.

# Rest of the World

1990–5

1    Shane Warne

2    Anil Kumble

3    Mushtaq Ahmed

4    Tim May

5    Venkatapathy Raju

6    Narendra Hirwani

It has been a privilege to be around Test cricket at the time of SHANE WARNE's emergence as one of the greatest spin bowlers the world has ever seen. I cannot say I am sad that I have not played against him because it might have been something of an embarrassment, but it has been a delight to watch him, both as a bowler and as a character in the modern game. The art of spin bowling in general and leg-spin bowling in particular was in danger of extinction in the face of the fast bowling warheads, and the service Warne has done for cricket, not just in Australia but throughout the world, has been immeasurable. He is just about the complete leg-spin bowler with his repertoire of deliveries – a vicious leg break, a very well-disguised googly and a good top-spinner – and the whole array unfolds before your eyes every time he has the ball in his hand. I was surprised by his comparative lack of success in South Africa in 1993–4 because I did not think they would play him very well at all, but, apart from that, he has swept everyone, England included, before him. My only concern is that he has had to bowl an enormous number of overs and I just hope that the workload does not shorten his career. He needs to be looked after a bit better than he has been because he is a real entertainer. Considering the pressure he has been under, he has also handled himself very well. It is part of the Australian policy to make their cricketers media-friendly and this has certainly worked to Warne's advantage. England can learn from the example.

I do not think that any of us thought we would ever see another Australian side containing two specialist spinners when Lillee and Thomson were running riot in the 'seventies but, although he has not picked up anything like the same number of wickets as Warne, TIM MAY has been an important foil for him. He does not get the same amount of turn, of course, although he is a big spinner of the ball in his own right. From looking fairly innocuous when I first saw him bowl, he came into his own in the 'nineties and was a real force to be reckoned with. He is a very positive off-spinner who does not just look to bowl maidens to allow Warne to attack at the other end, but tries to take wickets as well. Unfortunately for Australia, he does have long-term injury problems and we will probably not see a lot more of him.

A complete contrast to Warne is offered by India's ANIL KUMBLE who is not a great spinner of the ball at all but bowls his leg breaks and googlies with such pace and accuracy that he is almost as big a handful for the batsmen. Having said that, I rather doubt whether he will continue to take wickets in Test cricket at the same rate as he did for Northamptonshire in 1995. I think he will suffer the same fate as one of his Indian predecessors, Bhagwat Chandrasekhar, who found that the more batsmen played against him, the less success he had. The England batsmen of a few years ago came to play Chandra very much as an off-spinner, letting the occasional leg-spinner which ripped away pass harmlessly outside the edge of the bat, and I think the world's best players will be able to combat Kumble in the same way. That takes nothing away from his achievements in the game so far. To pick up 105 wickets and take Northamptonshire so close to their first County Championship was a fantastic effort.

I am not sure that VENKATAPATHY RAJU or Rajesh Chauhan should be considered as exceptional spin bowlers, but in company with Kumble they have formed a trio which has certainly helped India back up the Test match rankings. Raju is a fairly orthodox left armer who does not get that much turn, although when the wickets are in his favour, particularly at home, he is capable of taking wickets. The Indian leg-spinner, NARENDRA HIRWANI, is also back in contention after fading out of Test cricket almost as spectacularly as he entered it. He made a sensational start by taking sixteen wickets on his debut against the West Indies at Madras in 1987–8 when he was only nineteen. Most countries played him easily enough after that, though, and he went back to the drawing board. Watch this space, as they say.

MUSHTAQ AHMED is another leg-spinner who has had to fight his way back after having his image somewhat dented by the arrival of Shane Warne. He was young enough to do it, however, and he made a successful return to the Pakistan side in 1995–6 when he was able to give the Aussies a taste of their own medicine. It was a great effort because he had bowled a phenomenal 952 overs for Somerset in 1995. It was far too many, but they simply did not have a seam bowler fit to take the field at times. Mushtaq does not have the same well-stocked armoury as Warne and his googly is much easier to pick, although he has a nice, bouncy run-up and has obviously learned a lot from watching his predecessor, Abdul Qadir. He does not yet have as many tricks as Qadir and tends to lose control when he begins to tire. That is when he needs a sympathetic captain to take him off before he gets taken apart.

## 1980–9

1   Abdul Qadir

2   Iqbal Qasim

3   John Bracewell

4   Bruce Yardley

5   Tauseef Ahmed

6   Stephen Boock

If Shane Warne had not appeared on the scene when he did, ABDUL QADIR would probably be accepted as the best leg-spinner of modern times. We first clapped eyes on him in Pakistan in 1977–8 and were immediately struck by his beautiful bounding run-up and high action, not to mention the loopy flight and well-disguised googly. There were a few flaws in his temperament, though, and he got himself into trouble in New Zealand in 1984–5, when he was sent home 'for disciplinary reasons', and again in the Caribbean in 1987–8 when US$1,000 was handed over in an out-of-court settlement after a barracker had been punched in Barbados. Abdul could also get very flustered when the umpires did not respond to the choral society appealing in unison for lbw decisions or bat-pad catches. He finished his Test career with 236 wickets, but they had cost him more than 32 runs each, which suggests that he was not always the match-winner some of the media made him out to be. I have to say that I did not have as many problems playing him as some of my supposed superiors in the England batting line-up. I was seen off a couple of times playing against him in Pakistan but, apart from that, I don't remember him getting me out too often.

Qadir had the support of two very consistent spin bowlers during this period, IQBAL QASIM, who took 171 wickets with his slow left arm, and TAUSEEF AHMED who picked up 93 with his off-breaks. Iqbal was not dissimilar to Australia's Ray Bright in that he rolled the ball out rather than giving it a big tweak, and he did not have much success in England. In fact I remember him best because of his defiance with the bat which got me into a bit of hot water at Edgbaston in 1979. I bowled him a bouncer and hit him in the mouth after he had been in for a while as nightwatchman and it got the scribes' pens scratching.

JOHN BRACEWELL did a good job for New Zealand over the years, bowling defensively for the most part while seamers like Hadlee, Chatfield, Cairns, Snedden, and the younger Bracewell, Brendon, operated at the other end. He was never a great wicket-taker but he was a very competitive cricketer and an important part of the New Zealand side in the early 'eighties. His approach to off-spinning was more English than Antipodean and he bowled with a fair degree of accuracy.

BRUCE YARDLEY, on the other hand, was very much in the Australian style, pitching the ball outside the off stump, getting plenty of bounce and enjoying a fair amount of success with 126 Test wickets at 31 apiece. He had a rather ungainly action at the end of quite a long run but he bowled very intelligently, particularly on his home ground at Perth in Western Australia where he made good use of the Fremantle Doctor, the strong breeze which puts in a call most afternoons. Like most of the spinners in an era dominated by fast bowlers, he had to do a lot of defensive bowling while the quicks had a breather.

I remember STEPHEN BOOCK because he made his Test debut against us at Wellington in 1977-8 when New Zealand beat England for the first time, and he went on to turn in several useful performances with his left-arm spin. He took five wickets at Auckland later on in that series and played a big part in New Zealand's success when they won their first series against us in 1983–4.

＊          ＊          ●          ＊          ＊

1970–9

1    Bishen Bedi

2    Lance Gibbs

3    Bhagwat Chandrasekhar

4    Erapally Prasanna

5    Intikhab Alam

6    Ashley Mallett

The early 'seventies were good years for Indian cricket, not least because they had four of the best spin bowlers in the world. The pick of them was undoubtedly BISHEN BEDI, instantly recognisable by his brightly coloured patka which was as familiar in England as it was in India from his days with Northamptonshire. He was the most classical of all left-arm spinners with his lovely, studied approach, high arm action and endearing habit of applauding any batsman who was good enough to get down the pitch and hit him back over his head. Not many were, because he was probably unique in his ability to flight the ball and tempt the batsman out of his ground. He could also spin the ball sharply on any surface and it was quite amazing to hear the gasps followed by the roars of a packed stadium in Calcutta or Bombay as they saw the ball turn almost at right angles from Bedi's arm. He finished up with 266 Test wickets, the most by any Indian bowler until Kapil Dev came along.

Not far behind Bedi with 242 wickets came BHAGWAT CHANDRASEKHAR, whom I have already mentioned in connection with Anil Kumble. He had a very strange technique because his right arm had been withered by polio when he was a child and he needed a long run-up and a whirling action just to get the ball down to the other end at any kind of pace. It worked so well that he could be very nippy indeed and I can recall a few occasions when he was pacy enough to knock the stumps out of the ground. I can also remember batting against him at Madras in 1976–7 when the ball reared off a length and hit me under the chin. It showed how much pace he could generate on a quick wicket, and that Madras wicket was one of the fastest I have come across in Test cricket. Chandra did not turn his leg break all that much but he certainly spun his googly which often went very quickly indeed to have batsmen caught off bat and pad. He was a real match-winner and bowled India to two of their most famous victories – their first Test wins in England in 1971 and Australia in 1977–8.

As if Bedi and Chandra did not provide enough spin bowling for any side, India also had two world-class off-spinners in ERAPALLY PRASANNA and Srinivas Venkataraghavan. Prasanna was by far the bigger spinner of the ball, getting such an extraordinary amount of turn that questions were asked about his action in the early stages of his career. I never thought that he threw the ball, although, come to think of it, he always wore a shirt with long sleeves which were rolled up just below the elbow. Prasanna took 179 Test wickets but he was always a much more difficult proposition at home than he was abroad. The cold weather was a big disadvantage to the Indian spinners when they came to England at the start of the summer and he seemed to suffer from it more than most. It did not seem to be so much of a problem for Venkat who picked up 189 wickets in his three seasons with Derbyshire as well as taking 156 in Test cricket. He had to play second fiddle to Prasanna for a long time but while he did not spin the ball as much he probably had a bit more control.

The reason why Venkat does not figure in my 'six of the best' for this period is because India did not exactly have a monopoly of world-class spin bowlers. There were a few more around and none of them was better than my old friend, LANCE GIBBS. We played a lot of cricket together and shared a flat for a while when we were with Warwickshire and I found him to be an amazing character as well as an amazing bowler. His run-up, if you could call it that, was a model of economy and he used his extraordinarily long fingers to spin the ball right down around the knuckle rather than at the top of his finger. He made a huge contribution to West Indian cricket, particularly in the era between Hall and Griffith, which came to an end in the mid-'sixties, and the emergence of a new breed of quicks ten years later. The West Indies had some fairly modest seam bowlers around that time but Lance was always a threat at the other end. He kept going for seventy-nine Test matches and it was only right that he should put his name among the greats in the '300 Club' before he called it a day.

I was also lucky enough to play county cricket with INTIKHAB ALAM during my three years with Surrey. He was another excellent bowler with most of the attributes of a top-class leg-spinner as well as being a hard-hitting batsman who once scored 138 in a Test match against England. He had a lovely, high-stepping approach to the wicket, imparted real spin on the ball and bowled a very well-disguised googly.

Ian Chappell always makes sure that ASHLEY MALLETT gets plenty of credit when he talks about his great Australian sides of the 'seventies. He was not a prolific wicket-taker but he was a very steady off-spin bowler in all kinds of conditions. He bowled a typically Australian line outside the off stump to a predominantly offside field and offered a complete contrast to the English off-spinners of his time. Unfortunately we saw a lot more of Lillee, Thomson and Walker than we did of Mallett, although even when they were bowling he made his contribution by clinging to some breathtaking catches in the gully.

1970–95

1    Shane Warne

2    Bishen Bedi

3    Lance Gibbs

4    Bhagwat Chandrasekhar

5    Anil Kumble

6    Erapally Prasanna

✱     ✱     ●     ✱     ✱

All-time

1    Clarrie Grimmett

2    Bill O'Reilly

3    Shane Warne

4    Bishen Bedi

5    Lance Gibbs

6    Bhagwat Chandrasekhar

We could argue for ever about who was the better of the two great Australian leg-spinners, CLARRIE GRIMMETT or BILL O'REILLY – and whether SHANE WARNE is already better than either of them. LANCE GIBBS separates the contrasting Indian wizards, BISHEN BEDI and BHAGWAT CHANDRASEKHAR.

# 6

# SEAM AND SWING BOWLERS

## England

1990–5

1  Angus Fraser

2  Neil Foster

3  Gladstone Small

4  Phillip DeFreitas

5  Mark Ilott

6  Phil Newport

With the fast bowling cupboard almost bare, England have had to lean heavily on their seam and swing bowlers in recent times and few have looked more capable of carrying the burden than ANGUS FRASER. Before he developed a horrendous hip injury on the 1990–1 tour of Australia, 'Gus' was just what every captain wants in his side. You need reliable seamers and he was very accurate, with a nagging length and the ability to get extra bounce. He was also a tremendous trier who got very upset if he was hit for four – unlike one or two of his contemporaries who we will come to later. It was a tragedy for England when he picked up that injury, probably caused because Graham Gooch had so much faith in him that he tended to overbowl him on those hard Australian pitches. For a while, it threatened his career, and it was typical of the man that he came back well enough to take a career-best 8 for

75 in England's famous victory over the West Indies in Barbados in 1994.

I was England captain and as such responsible for picking NEIL FOSTER to make his Test debut against New Zealand at Lord's in 1983 with only nineteen first-class matches for Essex behind him. He had already had major surgery on his back which was held together by screws and various other bits of metal, and although he did not make a particularly auspicious start he was obviously a good bowler. He had an easy run up to the wicket, a nice, high action and he could get the ball to move around on most surfaces. He lacked a yard of pace to be devastating in Test match cricket but on county pitches where there was some assistance for him he picked up plenty of wickets. He bowled a lot of overs for Essex, probably too many for his slender frame, and it took him a while to establish himself in the England side. It was not until after my retirement in 1984 that he produced his finest performance – a match-winning 11 for 163 against India at Madras – and he had still not really fulfilled his potential when he joined the 'rebel' tour of South Africa in 1989–90 and was banned for three years. He played in just one more Test against Australia at Lord's in 1993 but by then his injury problems had returned to haunt him and he retired at the end of that season.

GLADSTONE SMALL was just a schoolboy when David Brown, then Warwickshire's manager, took him on to the professional staff at Edgbaston, and I got to know him well as he made fantastic strides in the game. His action was obviously restricted by the fact that he had been born without two vertebrae in his neck but, despite that, he had a good, economical run-up and could bowl at a decent pace in his early days. It looked as though he was going to cement a place in the England side for a long time to come when he clinched the Ashes for Mike Gatting with a match-winning 5 for 48 at Melbourne in 1986–7, but he had an unhappy time in Australia under Graham Gooch four years later and was hardly seen again at Test level. Only a few months earlier, he had bowled well in the Caribbean where he and Angus Fraser gave Gooch control while Devon Malcolm bowled very quickly at the other end. I felt that Gladstone should have played in more than seventeen Test matches but, like John Lever before him, he was probably too nice a guy for his own good. It is sometimes too easy to leave people like them out of the side.

In the same way as I got an early insight into Phil Tufnell's character, I was able to have a close look at PHILLIP DeFREITAS when I managed the England Under-19 side in the Caribbean and I am afraid that I came to much the same conclusion. He was a gifted all-round cricketer but his temperament was not sound enough to withstand the pressures of playing at Test level. He made an impressive start to his Test career when he was picked for the 1986-7 tour of Australia at the age of twenty and played his part in England's first Test victory at Brisbane, and he has had a couple of good spells since. In 1991, he took twenty-two wickets in the series against the West Indies and in 1994 he picked up thirty in the two series against New Zealand and South Africa. Overall, however, he has been a disappointment as a top-line competitor. His bowling is inconsistent, the line not accurate enough and the length just too short.

The England selectors have been very patient with MARK ILOTT, and he has yet to prove that he has the priceless ability of his Essex mentor, the aforementioned John Lever, to swing the ball into the right-hand batsmen and cut it away from them off the pitch. He has benefited from the experience of four England A tours and although he seems a lot stronger than he used to be he is still very prone to injury. It looked as though he might have put his problems behind him when he was virtually carrying the modest Essex seam attack in 1995 but he broke down again on the winter tour of South Africa.

PHIL NEWPORT has not had much luck either, in his four Test matches, the last of them in 1990-1 when he was flown out to Australia as a replacement. He does have the ability to swing the ball and is probably a better bowler now than he was then. His problem is that he does not have enough pace to trouble top-class batsmen, as we saw at Headingley in 1989 when he took a terrible pounding from the Australians.

Of the rest, Alan Igglesden just does not have the steel to be an England bowler, even Kent having difficulty getting him on to the field and committing himself to bowling for them. I was one of Micky Stewart's 'advisers' for a couple of weeks when he first took over as England manager and I went to watch Igglesden bowl against Derbyshire at Dartford. Sod's law will always apply on these occasions and Devon Malcolm looked a far better bowler than Igglesden did. When he got it right in county cricket, he had a nice, natural outswinger which was too good for some of the mediocre batsmen around, but when he got to Test level it was all a bit too much for him. As for Andrew Caddick, he had a meteoric rise through Somerset's ranks when he first arrived from New Zealand as a much-acclaimed Richard Hadlee lookalike. However, you could not say that when the going got tough he really got going. He had one or two good spells for England but one never got the impression that he was going to bowl a side out and when the wickets were flat he looked pretty innocuous.

*    *    ●    *    *

1980–9

1    Chris Old

2    Neil Foster

3    John Lever

4    Paul Allott

5    Robin Jackman

6    Richard Ellison

It is worth comparing and contrasting the Test match records of Chris Old, Mike Hendrick and John Lever who, together with Botham and Willis, provided England with almost an embarrassment of riches in the seam bowling department in the 'seventies and early 'eighties.

|  | Tests | Wkts | Avge | 5w | 10w |
|---|---|---|---|---|---|
| Mike Hendrick | 30 | 87 | 25.83 | – | – |
| John Lever | 21 | 73 | 26.72 | 3 | 1 |
| Chris Old | 46 | 143 | 28.11 | 4 | – |

CHRIS OLD was obviously the most talented of the three and would have achieved more than he did but for a slightly flawed temperament. He had such a history of injury which often seemed to afflict him just before a Test match that you sometimes wondered whether he wanted to play at all. The strange thing about it was that once you actually got him out on the park he very rarely threw in the towel. Indeed his commitment sometimes went beyond the call of duty, as it did against New Zealand at Wellington in 1977–8 when he bowled all day into the teeth of a gale to finish with 6 for 54. He was an amazingly gifted bowler, capable of swinging and seaming the ball in any direction and, especially in his early days, bowling very quickly, too. Ask the 1974 Indians who were hopping about all over the place when he was taking 18 wickets at only 13 runs apiece in the three-Test series, including a match-winning 5 for 21 at Lord's. He was still going strong in 1981 when he played important parts in our dramatic victories over the Australians at both Headingley and Edgbaston before his decision to join the 'rebel' tour of South Africa in 1981–2 signalled the end of his Test career.

MIKE HENDRICK had played his last Test match in 1980 which is why I have only included him in my next list but I will deal with him here because it is interesting to compare him with Old. He was another high-class fast-medium bowler with a lovely side-on action, great accuracy, a nagging, old-fashioned seamer's length and enough pace to force the batsmen on to the back foot. The trouble was that, having got them there, he really needed to pitch the ball a foot or so further up to cause the better players any serious problems. This was the great difference between Old and Hendrick. 'Chilly' knew the length to bowl at top-class batsmen; 'Hendo' tended to be perhaps half a yard too short. It helps to explain why he did not manage to pick up one five-wicket haul in his thirty Test matches, although he did bowl quite superbly for England at times, particularly on the 1978–9 tour of Australia when he took 19 wickets in the series at only 15 runs each.

JOHN LEVER – or 'JK' to everybody in the game – should certainly have played in more than twenty-one Test matches although he was clearly past his best when he was recalled against India at Headingley in 1986 at the age of thirty-seven. He still took six wickets in the match, which was typical of a bowler who had everything going for him that Chris Old did not when it came to commitment and getting out on to the field even if he was not a hundred per cent fit. He had been brought up in a tough school at Essex where they only had thirteen or fourteen on the staff and players were expected to turn up and play. Even when he was not in the England side, he was a tremendous team man and tourist, always willing to put himself out in the role of twelfth man and never failing to keep everyone's spirits up when he had every justification for being as miserable as anybody. He came into his own with his high-class left-arm swing bowling on the 1976–7 tour of India when he took 26 wickets at 14.61 in the series, including match figures of 10 for 71 on his debut at Delhi. The Indians tried to tarnish his performance with some ridiculous allegations about our using Vaseline to help the ball swing but they were completely false. The truth is that our physiotherapist, Bernard Thomas, had the idea of putting Vaseline-coated gauze on our eyebrows to stop the sweat running into our eyes in the fierce humidity, but the Indians chose to interpret it differently. I can assure the cricket world that John Lever was not trying to shine a cricket ball with Vaseline. There are much better substances to use than that.

PAUL ALLOTT could consider himself unlucky to be up against the likes of Old, Hendrick and Lever in the early stages of his career because he was not quite in that sort of company as a bowler although he did a creditable job for England in his thirteen Test matches and was very rarely embarrassed. He also struggled a bit with injuries, and while he was not alone in that, it was usually at an inappropriate time as far as his Test career was concerned. He had a good run-up and got close to the stumps to bowl wicket to wicket so that with any help at all from the pitch he could be a dangerous customer, but he did not have quite enough pace to get to the top at Test level.

I had close links with ROBIN JACKMAN not just because we started our cricket careers together at The Oval but also because it was my injury which led to his being called to the West Indies as a replacement in 1981 and set off the chain of events which almost resulted in the tour being cancelled because of his South African connections. I remember talking to him in 1971 about which one of us was going to leave Surrey because it was obvious that we were not going to play together in the same side. Apart from Geoff Arnold, they used to play Stewart Storey as the all-rounder and the two spinners, Intikhab Alam and Pat Pocock, so there was only room for one of us. In the end, I said that I would go because Robin was two years nearer a benefit than I was, so it was ironic that we finished up having our benefits in the same year – 1981. 'Jackers' was a great team man and a wholehearted trier who should have made a bigger impact for England than he did. I made a mistake as captain on the 1982–3 tour of Australia by preferring the younger blood of Norman Cowans and Derek Pringle, with the result that Robin did not play in any of the Test matches. With hindsight, it would have been better playing him because while he did not have any great pace he had good control and that was what we were lacking.

RICHARD ELLISON did as much as anybody to regain the Ashes from Australia in 1985 with a quite sensational performance in the Edgbaston Test. Having taken 6 for 77 in Australia's first innings, including a spell of 4 for 15, he took 4 for 1 in the second innings to reduce them to 36 for 5. Seven more wickets at The Oval meant that he had taken 17 in two Tests at only 10 runs each, but he found it much tougher in the Caribbean the following winter. If the ball did not swing, he was just the right pace to wallop around the ground and with his confidence in tatters he was soon drifting in and out of the Kent side. It was sad to see his career in such rapid decline because he was a talented swing bowler who got close to the stumps, used his front arm well and made the ball move around in most conditions in England. It was a more difficult task, as some of our younger brethren have found, trying to get the ball to swing in the Caribbean.

\*     \*     ●     \*     \*

1970–9

1    Chris Old

2    Geoff Arnold

3    Mike Hendrick

4    John Lever

5    Bob Cottam

6    Mike Selvey

There have been few better bowlers in English conditions than GEOFF ARNOLD. He did not enjoy touring very much because he just did not like being away from home and, not surprisingly, he was never as effective abroad, although in England he was as dangerous as anyone I have seen in twenty-five years. He was not particularly quick, but he was a very strong man and well capable of forcing a batsman on to the back foot with a surprise bouncer. Above all, though, G. G. Arnold – or 'Horse' to his friends – was a beautiful exponent of the art of seam bowling. The ball would invariably hit the seam before nipping away and I have a vivid memory of the 1972 England side dropping three catches off successive balls as they tried desperately to cling on to the many edges that found their way towards the slip cordon. For all his aversion to touring, he bowled uncomplainingly in tough conditions all over the world, but despite having a degree of success, including 6 for 45 against India at Delhi in 1972–3, he never relished the experience.

BOB COTTAM was a very versatile bowler who went on a couple of tours to the subcontinent between 1968 and 1973. He was capable of swinging the ball, seaming it and cutting it, but as I have said more than once, you need that little bit of extra pace to get Test batsmen out on good pitches and he was not quite quick enough. A controversial character who is not afraid to speak his mind, he knows a lot about the technical side of getting a cricket ball from one end of the pitch to the other and has become an excellent bowling coach.

MIKE SELVEY was never going to frighten anyone with his pace, either, but he certainly shook up the West Indians when he made his debut against them at Old Trafford in 1976. Called up at the last minute because of injuries, he proceeded to remove Fredericks, Richards and Kallicharran with his first twenty balls. He only played in two more Tests, one of them when Chris Old – surprise, surprise – was ill, although he was a good, honest county professional. Another bright bloke who now makes his living as a journalist, he had excellent control off a short run, knew what he was trying to do with the ball and could usually get some movement even off the flattest surface.

1970–95

1   Chris Old

2   Geoff Arnold

3   Angus Fraser

4   Mike Hendrick

5   Neil Foster

6   John Lever

All-time

1   Alec Bedser

2   Sydney Barnes

3   Maurice Tate

4   Chris Old

5   Geoff Arnold

6   Angus Fraser

ANGUS FRASER, at his best, edges into this list after two of my contemporaries, CHRIS OLD and GEOFF ARNOLD. ALEC BEDSER was the greatest exponent of seam and swing England has had although SYDNEY BARNES (189 wickets at 16) and MAURICE TATE (155 at 26) also had outstanding Test records.

\*     \*     ●     \*     \*

## Rest of the World

1990–5

1    Bruce Reid

2    Glenn McGrath

3    Paul Reiffel

4    Kenneth Benjamin

5    Javagal Srinath

6    Damien Fleming

One of the reasons why Australia have become such a dominant force in Test cricket recently is because their two world-class bowlers, Craig McDermott and Shane Warne, have been so well supported by the seam and swing merchants, no fewer than four of whom appear in this list.

They would have been even more formidable if the best of them, BRUCE REID, had not been plagued by back trouble which seemed to have ended his Test career when he broke down for the umpteenth time after the first Test against the West Indies at Brisbane in 1992–3. Reid had picked up seven wickets in that match to take his haul to 113 in only twenty-seven Tests, so it is fairly obvious that the guy would have finished up as one of the top wicket-takers of all time if he had been able to maintain any sort of fitness. Standing 6ft 8in tall and built like a stick insect, he was always going to be prone to spinal injury and not the least remarkable thing about him was the way he kept coming back to bowl as well as he had done before. He had been out for two years when England went to Australia in 1990–1 but he took twenty-seven wickets in four Tests, thirteen of them at Melbourne, before pulling up again, this time with a callus on his foot. He was a master of swing and seam, left arm into the bargain, and very few batsmen were comfortable against him. He was quick enough himself to force batsmen on to the back foot whereupon he would completely hoodwink them by forcing them to play at wide balls outside the off stump. They would be terrified that the ball was going to swing into them late so they would play wider and wider at him, often with disastrous consequences. He was just about the perfect foil for a fast bowler in any Test line-up.

Since the departure of Reid, apparently for good this time, and his great-hearted partner, Merv Hughes, McDermott's best support has probably come from GLENN McGRATH, who got into the side against New Zealand and South Africa in 1993–4 and has been making steady progress ever since. He had a disappointing time against England the following winter but he has since bowled very well against the West Indies in the Caribbean and Pakistan and Sri Lanka at home. He bowls with great economy, not wasting the new ball by pitching it too short but saving the bouncer as a real surprise, and is quite prepared to wear batsmen down with his accuracy. Apart from that, anyone with his batting ability who does not mind sticking it up the West Indian fast bowlers must have something going for him. It was evident on that tour that the Australians had a specific ploy of keeping the ball up to the front-line batsmen but pitching it short to the tail-enders, and although McGrath cannot bat at all, he was quite happy to bowl short at the likes of Curtly Ambrose and Courtney Walsh. It worked, too. The quicks do not mind dishing it out but they are not so keen on facing it themselves and the last five wickets would regularly go down for very few runs.

Looks were certainly deceptive in the case of PAUL REIFFEL who only got into the Australian side in England in 1993 because Craig McDermott had gone home and Brendon Julian was injured. Until then, he had looked pretty innocuous, but he soon showed what a good bowler he is by taking eight wickets at Headingley in the match which made sure that Australia kept the Ashes, and another six at Edgbaston. Reiffel also played a big part in Australia's triumph in the West Indies in 1994–5 when no one gave them a chance after McDermott and Damien Fleming had broken down. Always very accurate, always making the batsman play the ball, he has the ability to move the ball off the seam and, in the right conditions, swing it a little bit as well.

Graham Gooch must have felt as though an old nightmare had returned to haunt him when he came across DAMIEN FLEMING on the 1994–5 Australian tour. Fleming, a genuine outswing bowler with the ability to cut the ball back off the pitch, had him in all sorts of trouble and at one stage got him out four times in successive innings in much the same way as Terry Alderman used to do. Injuries have taken their toll of him lately but he is definitely a talented bowler and one to watch if he can get his fitness back.

It is a moot point whether the West Indies' KENNETH BENJAMIN should be in the seam and swing section or among the genuine fast bowlers because he certainly tests the middle of the pitch. He is a much better bowler, however, when he pitches the ball up, as Michael Holding was constantly imploring him to do in England in 1995. He does not have a very pretty action but he is a powerful man with great physical strength in the delivery stride and the stamina to bowl long spells. He clearly has the edge over his namesake, Winston, although he seems to have joined him in falling foul of the West Indian authorities.

India's latest spearhead, JAVAGAL SRINATH, is another fast medium bowler who is capable of bowling some pretty rapid deliveries. He learned how it was done at the fast bowling academy that Dennis Lillee set up in Madras a few years ago and Courtney Walsh was sufficiently impressed to recommend him to Gloucestershire as his replacement in 1995 when he was touring with the West Indies. Srinath took eighty-seven wickets at only nineteen apiece and while we must take the quality of some of the county batting into account he clearly has great potential.

1980–9

1    Terry Alderman

2    Bruce Reid

3    Ewan Chatfield

4    Geoff Dymock

5    Manoj Prabhakar

6    Mike Whitney

TERRY ALDERMAN was the bane of many an English batsman's life in the 'eighties, whether he was playing for Australia or Kent. He was a master of seam and swing and English conditions suited him only too well as he demonstrated by taking a record forty-two Test wickets on the 1981 tour and picking up another forty-one in 1989. He might have done even more damage if he had not suffered a serious shoulder injury rugby-tackling a so-called England supporter who had run on to the ground at the start of the 1982–3 tour, and then joined a 'rebel' tour of South Africa after he had been selected for the 1985 Ashes campaign. He was a strong man with a good, controlled run-up and a high arm action and he got very close to the stumps to bowl wicket to wicket. This caused the batsmen, even those of the quality of Graham Gooch, enormous problems because it meant that if he got the ball to swing or cut away off the seam he had them caught behind or in the slips and if he did not he often trapped them lbw. He also had enough pace to make the batsman think that he should stay on the back foot and this made them very vulnerable as well. He finished up with 170 wickets in his forty-one Tests.

Compared with Alderman, EWAN CHATFIELD looked a fairly innocuous bowler but he did a great job for New Zealand as a foil to Richard Hadlee. What is more, he took 123 Test wickets himself, which was not a bad effort for a man who had to be given the kiss of life after being struck on the head by Peter Lever on his Test debut at Auckland in 1974–5. He went on to play Test cricket for another fourteen years, taking five wickets at Headingley in 1983 when New Zealand won for the first time in England and bowling very tightly in 1983–4 when they won their first series against us.

GEOFF DYMOCK was another under-rated bowler who served Australia well, particularly after they had been weakened by the mass exodus to Kerry Packer's World Series Cricket in the late 'seventies. He did not make much of an impression when he came to England in 1977 and failed to get into the Test side, but he showed us what he could do with his left-arm swing when we lost all three Tests in Australia in 1979–80. The Packer men were back by then; however, Dymock had done well in India and he more than justified his selection by taking seventeen wickets, including a match-winning 6 for 34 in the first Test at Brisbane. Only the great Lillee picked up more English wickets in that series.

MIKE WHITNEY had a fairly eventful start to his Test career when he was plucked out of league cricket to play against England at Old Trafford in 1981 and had the misfortune to be underneath a wicked skier which dropped to earth as Ian Botham blazed his way towards one of his most memorable centuries. He is probably still haunted by the memory, which he managed to put out of his mind long enough to bowl some useful spells for Australia, especially in one-day internationals. He was a genuine left-arm swing bowler with a bit of pace and the ability to move the ball into the right-hander although he tended to slant it across him rather than get it to seam away.

MANOJ PRABHAKAR, who also features in the all-rounders' section, has no pace to speak of but he does swing the ball and this has enabled him to make a decent fist of opening the bowling for India in the most unrewarding conditions, in support of first Kapil Dev and now Javagal Srinath. He is probably better suited to one-day cricket but he has picked up more than a hundred Test wickets which is not bad going for a player who can open the batting as well.

1970–9

1   Max Walker

2   Bob Massie

3   Ewan Chatfield

4   Dick Collinge

5   Gary Gilmour

6   Madan Lal

MAX WALKER – or 'Tangles' as they called him because of his
ungainly action in which he seemed to deliver the ball off the wrong
foot – was a very important cog in the Australian machine in the
'seventies. A very strong man with a huge upper torso, he had a
strange open-chested style which enabled him to swing the ball and
get it to nip around off the seam. And he was quick enough to force
them on to the back foot before having them groping forward
without quite getting to the pitch of the ball. As I have said before,
performances in the Caribbean are a good measure of a seam
bowler's ability, and Walker took twenty-six Test wickets there in
1972–3, but it was in support of Lillee and Thomson that he was
at his most effective. Batsmen looking to get some respite from their
thunderbolts felt that they could take liberties with him, but big
Max was not having any of that and they often lost their wickets
trying to force the pace against him.

I doubt if anyone has ever seen the like of BOB MASSIE's
amazing performance for Australia against England at Lord's in
1972 when he made the ball go round in circles to take eight
wickets in each innings. Only Jim Laker and Sydney Barnes have
taken more wickets in a Test match than he did as he swung the
ball four or five feet to beat players of the calibre of John Edrich
and Mike Smith when they were not offering a shot. He would set

the ball off well wide of the right-hander's leg stump at times and turn them round completely before knocking out the off stump or having them caught in the slips. As for the left-handers who saw the ball starting outside their off stump, I well remember John Edrich padding up to Massie at Trent Bridge and having his castle knocked over. The most extraordinary thing about it all was that the magic left him as abruptly as it had appeared. He took only seven wickets in the remaining three Tests of that series, eight more at home against Pakistan and his Test career was over, giving some credence to those cynics who suggested that lip salve might have been the magic ingredient which helped him to swing the ball so prodigiously. They may have thought so but I could not possibly comment.

Just as Bob Massie had devastated England with his right-arm swing in 1972, so GARY GILMOUR destroyed them with his left-arm variety in the semi-final of the first World Cup at Headingley in 1975. In fact he did not just swing the ball in the heavy atmosphere but moved it both ways off the seam to take 6 for 14 in his 12 overs as England were shot out for 93. Gilmour really made the ball talk that day; unfortunately he did not do it very often in a brief Test career which was badly disrupted by injury. He was never a very fit bloke, who had to compete for a place with the likes of Lillee, Thomson and Walker, and fifty-four Test wickets was scant reward for a bowler of his talent.

When he retired in 1978, DICK COLLINGE, another left-arm swing bowler, was New Zealand's leading wicket-taker with 116 in his thirty-five Test matches. He looked rather cumbersome with his inordinately long run, flailing arms and a delivery stride which seemed to take an awful lot out of him, although he was an effective bowler who struck the killer blows when we lost to New Zealand for the first time at Wellington. We only needed 137 to win but he got rid of Geoff Boycott, Derek Randall and Geoff Miller in his opening spell and we were all out for 64.

Bowlers of any pace on the subcontinent have to learn to swing the ball because there is hardly any movement off the seam, and two of the better exponents in the 'seventies were India's MADAN LAL who came back to take 5 for 23 at Bombay and give them the only victory of the otherwise barren 1981-2 series, and Pakistan's Asif Masood, who bowled very well in England in 1971.

1970–95

1    Terry Alderman

2    Bruce Reid

3    Max Walker

4    Glenn McGrath

5    Ewan Chatfield

6    Geoff Dymock

\*        \*                \*        \*

All-time

1    Alan Davidson

2    Bill Johnston

3    Fazal Mahmood

4    Terry Alderman

5    Bruce Reid

6    Max Walker

There are no fewer than five Australians in my all-time list, headed
by two great left-arm swing bowlers, ALAN DAVIDSON, who

could have been included in the all-rounder category, and BILL JOHNSTON, who could not. FAZAL MAHMOOD was good enough to be called 'Pakistan's Alec Bedser' and what TERRY ALDERMAN, BRUCE REID and MAX WALKER have done to England in recent times is only too fresh in the memory.

# 7

# WORST NUMBER ELEVENS

1970–95

1   Phil Tufnell

2   Alan Igglesden

3   Les Taylor

4   Devon Malcolm

5   Mike Hendrick

6   Norman Cowans

Having batted at number eleven for most of my Test career and achieved the not inconsiderable average of 11.50 (boosted, I have to admit, by fifty-five not outs), I feel I can speak with some authority on this subject. I have seen some shockers in my time, but anyone who can get DEVON MALCOLM promoted to number ten as PHIL TUFNELL did in Australia in 1994–5 deserves the accolade. Even ALAN IGGLESDEN was spared the indignity of batting after Devon in the Caribbean the previous winter although I could never quite see why. LES TAYLOR, who managed just one run in his brief Test career, was unchallenged for the final berth, as were MIKE HENDRICK and NORMAN COWANS. They even got me promoted.

## Rest of the World

1     Ehtesham-ud-Din

2     Alan Hurst

3     Jim Higgs

4     Bhagwat Chandrasekhar

5     Maninder Singh

6     Lance Gibbs

Pride of place must go to EHTESHAM-UD-DIN, the portly Pakistani who put in a cameo performance at the Headingley Test in 1992. He had been summoned from the Bolton Association side, Daisy Hill, where he was due to play in his own benefit match, to take the new ball, only he never quite got round to it. He pulled a muscle in the field and limped off but not before he had made his customary duck. He scored just two runs in his five Test matches.

It was a pity he did not play more because he might have challenged the record of ALAN HURST, the Australian fast bowler, who contrived to make three 'pairs' in one season of Test cricket in 1978–9. Two of them were against England, although in one match he managed to get in ahead of JIM HIGGS, who was still trying to live down his experience in England in 1975 when he was bowled by the only ball he faced on the entire tour.

Two Indian spinners, MANINDER SINGH and BHAGWAT CHANDRASEKHAR, earned the right to come next by averaging 3.80 and 4.07 respectively in Test cricket and I have also included my old friend, LANCE GIBBS, because he would be offended if I didn't.

# 8

# ALL-ROUNDERS

## England

1990–5

1   Dominic Cork

2   Ian Botham

3   Chris Lewis

4   Derek Pringle

5   David Capel

6   Mike Watkinson

For the best part of two decades, every all-rounder selected to play for England seems to have been judged by the standards of IAN BOTHAM and that is palpably unfair. There has been no one good enough to lace the boots, never mind follow in the footsteps of a quite extraordinary cricketer who finished his Test match career in 1992 with 5,200 runs, 383 wickets and 120 catches. When you consider that the equally incomparable Sir Garfield Sobers is the only other player in Test history to have completed the treble of 1,000 runs,100 wickets and 100 catches, you get some idea of what a remarkable performer he was. I first came across Botham in 1976 when he played in the one-day international series against the West Indies, but it was during the Centenary Test at Melbourne the following winter that I got my first real insight into his character. He was out there on a scholarship playing for Melbourne University (some would say it was the nearest he was ever going to get to a university) and he spent a lot of time in the England dressing room telling anyone who cared to listen how much he was going to achieve in the game. He has been as good as his word. We knew he had the golden touch from the moment he persuaded Greg Chappell to drag the ball into his stumps in his very first Test match against Australia at Trent Bridge in 1977. It was not the last wicket he was going to get with a rank bad ball but there was a lot more to him than that as we were to discover that winter.

He did not play in a Test match on the first half of the tour in Pakistan after falling ill with dysentery but he was back in the rudest health by the time we got to New Zealand. We had suffered an embarrassing defeat in the first Test on a park pitch at Wellington where Geoffrey Boycott achieved the doubtful distinction of becoming the first England captain to lose to New Zealand and our leader was understandably twitchy during the second Test at Christchurch. Having just failed to enforce the follow-on, we needed some quick runs on the fourth day but they were not forthcoming from our openers, Boycott and Brian Rose, and the cause was not helped when Derek Randall was run out, backing up, without a warning, by Ewan Chatfield. As vice-captain, I decided to send Ian in to step up the scoring rate. He had already become only the second England player (after Tony Greig) to score a hundred and take five wickets in the same Test and now he made a pretty thorough job of increasing the scoring rate – not just with runs off his own bat but also by running out the captain! We then had to persuade Geoffrey to declare to give ourselves a chance of bowling New Zealand out. It took some doing but in the end we managed it and Ian and I picked up seven wickets between us as New Zealand were dismissed inside four hours.

The outrageous, adventurous Botham had arrived and from then on he was absolutely irresistible with a string of match-winning performances, including his tour de force against Australia in 1981. His best performances tended to be at home rather than abroad although he did have remarkable success in India's Golden Jubilee Test at Bombay in 1980 when he became the first player to score a century and take ten wickets in the same match. It was an extraordinary feat in searing heat – apparently without any sleep and only a large quantity of Johnnie Walker to keep him going!

The only problem with all this was that we came to rely on him too much. Mike Brearley certainly knew how to get the best out of him, although I felt that he bowled him too long at times. I remember one particular match at Perth when he bowled all day but for two overs into the wind. It was a superhuman effort, and I do think that the constant workload may have started the back trouble which was to plague him later in his career. He was a willing work-horse and just kept charging in, always believing that he was capable of taking wickets. More often than not he was right and he was still capable of bowling very quickly right up to 1985, when he produced one of his fastest spells against the Australians. He was never quite the same after that, however, his enforced absence from the game through a Test and County Cricket Board suspension and major back surgery sending his bowling into terminal decline. At the time I thought that he could continue to make the sparks fly by concentrating more on his batting and going in higher up the order and I was disappointed that this did not happen. He was still capable of doing a useful job for England opening the batting in one-day internationals, but I guess he needed the buzz of the Test match scene to bring the best out of him.

At least DOMINIC CORK seems to be made of the same stuff. It is far too early to start making comparisons, but Cork has made an even more spectacular start to his Test career than Botham did. He announced his arrival by taking 7 for 43 – the best figures by an England player on his debut – against the West Indies at Lord's in 1995 and two Test matches later at Old Trafford performed the first hat-trick by an England bowler for thirty-eight years. He also scored a Test match fifty and although he is still very much a bowler who can bat a bit, there is certainly a chance that his batting will develop. At the moment he is a bit jumpy at the crease and must give his partner kittens by feigning to go for a run every time he makes contact with the ball. He has real talent as a bowler, though, and he is a great competitor who is not afraid to give as good as he gets with both bat and ball. Just like Botham, in fact.

While Cork was touring South Africa, the enigmatic CHRIS LEWIS was hoping to start 1996 with his third county, Surrey, always assuming that he could prove his fitness, having left first Leicestershire and then Nottinghamshire in search of fulfilment. His problem seems to be a temperamental one. He has all the talent in the world, he is a magnificent mover and he has a brilliant eye – all of which are manifestly evident from his work in the field. Yet playing under pressure, which is what Test match cricket is all about, he has been found sadly wanting. The only times he has made big scores – and his 117 against India at Madras in 1992–3 springs readily to mind – have been when the pressure was off. Far too often the bowlers have not even had to get him out. He has got himself out by chipping the ball up to midwicket, mid-on or square leg. It is much the same story with the ball, although there were signs in Australia in 1994–5 that he could actually bowl well when the pressure was on. He had been fortunate to be added to the squad because of injury problems but he had a lot to do with a very good England victory in Adelaide. Unfortunately he could not capitalise on that performance because of the latest in a series of mysterious injuries and illnesses which have plagued his career.

Another under-achiever was DEREK PRINGLE. I was responsible for picking him in 1982 when he was still at Cambridge University and I always thought that he would produce more for England than he actually did. By the time he played in the last of his thirty Tests in 1992, his average of 15 with the bat and 35 with the ball would have looked better the other way round. He rarely contributed at all with the bat, despite batting at number seven or eight, and although his height (6ft 6in) gave him the ability to get bounce from a good length, one would have expected him to be able to bowl much quicker. I remember trying to get him to do that on his first tour to Australia in 1982–3 because at his pace he was not going to pose too much of a threat but he could not manage it. That was a shame because he was a very bright character and a deep thinker about the game – as he has shown since embarking on a new career as a cricket writer.

Geoffrey Boycott was always a great advocate of DAVID CAPEL although I could never really see where all his confidence and expectation came from. He is a gifted cricketer who should have been able to do a job for England, batting in the lower order and bowling a fair number of overs in a defensive mode. In fact he did bowl adequately at times on Graham Gooch's tour of the West Indies in 1990, although he did not score many runs and he was never quite good enough in either department to shine as a Test match player.

No one would have been more surprised than MIKE WATKINSON himself when he became England's latest all-rounder at the age of thirty-four – although he was primarily playing as an off-spinner on his debut against the West Indies at Old Trafford in 1995. He certainly gives the ball a tremendous tweak, but while he has the potential to be a wicket-taking bowler I doubt whether he will ever be a match-winning bowler in the fourth innings of a Test match. As a batsman, he does not look too pretty, but he can be effective, as he showed in making 82 not out at Trent Bridge. He also has guts, determination and a will to succeed – the very attributes which some of England's all-rounders of the period have lacked.

1980–9

1    Ian Botham

2    Peter Willey

3    Derek Pringle

4    Geoff Miller

5    David Capel

6    Ian Greig

With such a larger-than-life character as Ian Botham dominating this period it was very difficult for any of the other England all-rounders to get much of a look-in, but PETER WILLEY made some important contributions, particularly against the West Indies who he faced in fifteen of his twenty-six Test matches. He was never going to take wickets on a regular basis with his off-spinners at Test level so he was basically a batsman who could bowl a bit. And what a brave batsman he was. His name was always the first on the list whenever England came across the men from the Caribbean and he had some memorable duels, particularly with the menacing Colin Croft. He had an extraordinary stance, so open that he almost seemed to be facing the square leg umpire and that must have put the fast bowlers' backs up straight away. Not that it ever seemed to bother 'Will', who always appeared to be giving the maximum amount of whatever ability he had. Tremendous application, professionalism and a sheer love of the game are what got him where he did. It was no surprise that when he took up umpiring he made a good fist of that as well.

From the moment that GEOFF MILLER made his Test debut against the West Indies in 1976 until his last appearance against them in 1984, a succession of England selectors and captains, myself included, felt that he was going to be a worthwhile all-rounder. Unfortunately his final figures – 1,213 runs at 25, 60 wickets at 30 – suggested that he was lucky to play in as many Tests (thirty-four) as he did. He did bat reasonably well at times and I recall being the last man out when he was left stranded on 98 against Pakistan at Lahore in 1977–8. He equalled that score against India at Old Trafford in 1982 but the fact that he made only two centuries in his entire first-class career was a travesty for a player of his ability. He had his moments with the ball, too, and was England's most successful bowler on the 1978–9 tour of Australia when he took twenty-three wickets in our 5–1 victory, yet even then you never really got the impression that he was going to bowl sides out. Still, it was always good to have him around because he was a terrific tourist. Before Allan Lamb appeared on the scene, he was often given the onerous task of rooming with Ian Botham and they became known as 'Higgs and Hill, the demolition experts'. Dusty is now making a large part of his living as an after-dinner speaker and it is interesting and, I think, quite revealing that the whole tone of his performance is a parody of how little he achieved in the game.

Another of the rabbits that I pulled out of the hat during my time as captain was IAN GREIG. I do not mean that he was a rabbit in the cricketing sense, but he was never going to emulate the exploits of his elder brother, Tony. It was just that with fifteen players banned for playing in South Africa we did have to scrape the barrel. And, to be fair to Ian, his figures of 4 for 53 on his debut against Pakistan in 1982 did match those of Tony in his first Test.

\*          \*          ●          \*          \*

1970–9

1    Ian Botham

2    Tony Greig

3    Basil D'Oliveira

4    Ray Illingworth

5    Geoff Miller

6    Richard Hutton

It was just as well for England that IAN BOTHAM arrived on the scene when he did because there was a gaping hole to fill following the defection of TONY GREIG to Kerry Packer's World Series Cricket. Greig's influence on English cricket as a player, as a captain and as an arch-plotter in the revolution which split the game must never be underestimated. As an all-rounder, which is what we are mainly concerned with here, he was inspirational, whether he was batting, bowling or fielding superbly in the slips. As a batsman, he was quite outrageous at times, especially when he was signalling fours to the baying Australian crowds after he had boomed Lillee and Thomson to the boundary and then ducking theatrically under the vengeful bouncer next ball. He was the first of the modern batsmen to adopt the 'stand and deliver' stance which was probably more comfortable for a man standing 6ft 7in tall and was all very well until someone like Michael Holding was firing ninety mph yorkers under his bat. He was at his best when he was playing his shots, yet of the many great innings he played for England the one that sticks in my memory defied all his attacking instincts. It was against India at Calcutta in 1977 when he got up from his sick bed and went out to bat for almost seven hours to set up a victory which went a long way towards winning the series. Three years before that, Greig had almost caused a riot in Trinidad by running out Alvin Kallicharran after the last ball of the day had been bowled, but I prefer to remember his truly magnificent bowling performance in the last match of that series, also in Trinidad. England had gone into it with Geoff Arnold and Greig to open the bowling and Pat Pocock, Jack Birkenshaw and Greig again to bowl off-spin. And it was Greig who won the match by taking thirteen wickets. Ironically, that victory kept Mike Denness in his job as captain until Greig took over in 1975. I think he would have held it for a long time after that if Packer had not dangled the carrot of World Series Cricket in front of him. Some would say that he sold his soul to Packer; others would say that cricket does not evolve unless there are revolutions in the game – and add that the English game is ready for another revolution instead of just meandering along in its cosy, county thinking.

If you ever wanted to ignite the BASIL D'OLIVEIRA powder keg, all you had to do was suggest that Tony Greig was a better all-rounder than he was, so I had better keep my head down when he sees this list. I had the pleasure of sharing a room with Basil after I joined the 1970–1 tour of Australia and I could only marvel at his constitution. You would have thought that he and Ian Botham were related from that point of view since late nights and a few drinks were very much on their menus. It was not the only thing they had in common. Basil was a top-class all-rounder in his own right, a batsman capable of averaging 40 in Test matches and a genuine swing bowler. Many of Raymond Illingworth's England sides had D'Oliveira at number five, Illingworth himself at six and Alan Knott at seven, which shows how much responsibility the all-rounders had. Basil was a poor starter but he was an immensely strong man and it showed in his ability to play so convincingly on the onside. As a bowler, he could get the ball to wobble about in most atmospheric conditions. He used to bowl a very tight line, always attacking the off stump or just outside it where he picked up a lot of wickets, either caught behind or in the slips. We never knew quite how old he was when he was performing these feats, although we always suspected that he was a few years older than the record books said, which made them all the more remarkable.

RAYMOND ILLINGWORTH began his playing career as an off-spinner and finished it as a hugely influential captain; when he was batting at number six for England he was definitely an all-rounder and a pretty useful one as well. He was not a particularly attractive batsman to watch, but he was good enough to score two Test centuries and he thrived on his responsibility as captain. He was also an excellent bowler and although he was criticised for putting himself on at the right time and at the right ends, not all of that criticism was justified. I well remember the seventh and last Test of the 1970–1 Australian tour. We had got to the final day of the longest series in Test history with Australia needing 100 runs with five wickets in hand to prevent us from regaining the Ashes. Everybody expected the seamers to do the bowling because they had picked up most of the early wickets but Illingworth took the responsibility, put himself on and struck the crucial blows. It was typical of the man.

Another all-rounder from Yorkshire, RICHARD HUTTON, played in a few Test matches at the start of the 'seventies. He had been an outstanding schoolboy player, but, like young Liam Botham is doing today, he carried an enormous burden of expectancy in following in the footsteps of a famous father. Richard did grow up into a decent county cricketer; however, apart from one innings of 81 against India, he never suggested that he would be able to hold his own at Test level.

1970–95

1   Ian Botham
2   Tony Greig
3   Basil d'Oliveira
4   Ray Illingworth
5   Dominic Cork
6   Peter Willey

\*      \*      ●      \*      \*

All-time

1   Ian Botham
2   Wilfred Rhodes
3   Tony Greig
4   Maurice Tate
5   Trevor Bailey
6   Basil d'Oliveira

Three of the great all-rounders I had the privilege of playing with are joined by WILFRED RHODES, the legendary Yorkshire left-arm spinner who partnered Jack Hobbs in a record opening stand, MAURICE TATE, who began his career as a batsman and became one of England's finest bowlers, and TREVOR BAILEY, the fast-medium bowler who was a hero in many a batting crisis.

\*          \*          ●          \*          \*

### Rest of the World

1990–5

1   Steve Waugh

2   Brian McMillan

3   Sir Richard Hadlee

4   Kapil Dev

5   Imran Khan

6   Wasim Akram

The early 'nineties saw the retirements of three of the greatest all-rounders in the history of the game and I guess we could argue for ever over the order in which we should rate them.

Personally, I do not think you could ask for a much better all-round cricketer than SIR RICHARD HADLEE. When we first saw him in England in 1973 he had an enormous run-up and his bowling was pretty wayward, but once he developed that short, beautifully rhythmic approach through playing Sunday League cricket for Nottinghamshire, he became just about the perfect seam bowler. His brilliant control of length and line, tantalisingly short of a length on or outside off stump, coupled with his ability to seam the ball away from the right-hander, more often than not gave the wicketkeeper and slips an absolute field day. It was amazing how much pace he could generate from that short run and relatively frail body, but he was very wiry and had a lovely wrist action, which is so important to the quick bowler. He finished up with 431 Test wickets and although his most devastating performances were against Australia – including 9 for 52 and 6 for 71 at Brisbane in 1985–6 – I remember him best for his contributions to New Zealand's most famous victories over England. He took 10 for 100 (6 for 26 in the second innings) in their first Test win over us at Wellington in 1977–8, and although he did not get a single wicket when they beat us in England for the first time in 1983, he scored an invaluable 75 not out in their first innings. As a batsman, he had his problems with the short ball, and Ian Botham, for one, always fancied getting him out with it. It did not work very often, though, because he had his own peculiar way of coping with it and I recall him making 99 off 81 balls on a terrible pitch at Christchurch in 1983–4 when Ian thought he was bowling bouncers and Richard treated them like long hops. He was not a particularly sociable character but I think he would admit that he owed a debt to English cricket. I find it intriguing that since people like Hadlee, Geoff Howarth and John Wright, all of whom benefited from playing county cricket, disappeared from the scene, New Zealand have struggled at Test level.

Like Hadlee, IMRAN KHAN still had a lot to learn when he first appeared in English cricket in 1971, playing for both Worcestershire and Pakistan as a very raw nineteen-year-old who bowled fairly innocuous inswingers and did not seem to have any great pretensions with the bat. But what a fast learner he was. Within three years he was scoring two centuries in a match for Oxford University against Nottinghamshire and two years after that his hostile fast bowling was giving Pakistan their first victory in Australia. He had realised what hard work it was trying to bowl quick on unresponsive pitches and got himself very fit for the job. He also made himself into a very useful batsman indeed and from then on he was the dominant figure in Pakistan cricket, crowning a glorious career by leading them to their World Cup triumph over Graham Gooch's England side at Melbourne in 1992. He was a devastating new-ball bowler who could get the ball to swing in all kinds of conditions, but my main recollection is of his hostility towards the England tail-enders, myself included, at Edgbaston in 1982. Bob Taylor and I batted for a long time against him in a last wicket stand of 79 which paved the way for our 113-run victory. Imran peppered us with so many bouncers that I actually missed the next Test at Lord's with a stiff neck, caused by having to take so much evasive action. To make matters worse, we lost that match, but I was back at Headingley where we won by three wickets to complete one of my most satisfying series as captain. Pakistan had an extremely strong side and I thought it was a very good performance to beat them with a team weakened by the unavailability of our South African 'rebels'.

Earlier that summer we had beaten India despite the efforts of KAPIL DEV, who had added a new dimension to Indian cricket from the moment he appeared on the Test match scene in 1978–9. For years their attack had been led by little seamers like Abid Ali and Eknath Solkar, Madan Lal and Karsan Ghavri, whose main job was to get a bit of shine off the ball before the spinners took over for the rest of those long, hot days under the burning sun. Kapil was a genuine new-ball bowler who approached the wicket on a lovely bouncy run and got very close to the stumps before delivering his natural outswinger. That, combined with his refusal to be intimidated by the most unrewarding pitches in the world for a quick bowler, was to bring him more Test wickets than anyone else in the history of the game. He was also a swashbuckling batsman with a brilliant array of shots, although the lofted extra cover drive was his speciality. He was never afraid to go down the wicket and hit the spinners back over their heads and he was seen at his best at Lord's in 1990 when India, at 430 for 9, needed 24 to avoid the follow-on. Kapil did it by driving Eddie Hemmings for four successive sixes, something which no one had ever done before in a Test match against Eddie or anyone else. Lord's was also the scene of two of his greatest triumphs as India's captain – the stunning World Cup Final victory over the West Indies in 1983, and their first win over England there three years later. Whether he was captain or not – and that was often at the whim of the Indian authorities, whose political machinations sometimes matched even those of Pakistan – Kapil always gave of his best and it is hard to believe that his record of 434 Test wickets will ever be broken. I guess Shane Warne has a chance of doing it, although he is going to have to play for a long time to catch up with Kapil.

All of these three great all-rounders were first and foremost bowlers who were capable of great deeds with the bat, but my number one in this five-year period is essentially a batsman who can make a vital contribution with the ball. In fact STEVE WAUGH is a good enough batsman to have joined his twin brother, Mark, in my 'six of the best' in the middle-order, and after a long period when his bowling was affected by back trouble he has re-emerged as a genuine all-rounder. Few people gave Australia a chance when they went to the West Indies in 1994–5 and lost their two strike bowlers, Craig McDermott and Damien Fleming, and had to rely on Glenn McGrath, Paul Reiffel and Brendon Julian to do the bulk of the bowling. Steve Waugh made up the difference in the fourth seamer's role as well as batting with great distinction and was one of the main reasons why Australia can now claim to be the champions of Test cricket. His critics have often accused him of not fancying quick bowling – can anyone put their hand on their heart and say that they do fancy it? Steve has occasionally been exposed by naked pace, but over the years he has been one of the most convincing batsmen against the West Indies. He plays very well square of the wicket on the offside and, when the ball is not seaming around, he punishes the bowlers through midwicket in typical Australian style. He is also a very accurate bowler who has clearly benefited from playing a lot of one-day cricket. He is often given the responsibility of bowling at the death, when he is well capable of bowling five yorkers out of six, and, more than anybody perhaps, he has learned the art of changing his pace. Apart from using it to great effect in the one-day game, he has brought the same skill into Test cricket and dismissed seemingly well-established batsmen who have mistimed shots to be caught at either mid-off or mid-on. He always looks a bit surly and grumpy on the field and has certainly not endeared himself to England's players in recent years, but he is an intensely competitive character. He takes his cricket very seriously indeed – as do most of the 'new' Australians – and he is rightly proud of the fact that he has fought his way into the side and held his place in bad times as well as good.

While I rate Steve Waugh as today's leading all-rounder, he is facing a real challenge from BRIAN MCMILLAN, the powerful South African who at his current rate of progress could finish up with the best record of them all. When England toured South Africa in 1995–6, he was averaging over 40 with the bat and under 30 with the ball and I cannot find an all-rounder in the history of the game who managed to sustain those figures in a career of more than twenty Test matches. We saw him briefly at Warwickshire in 1986 when he was signed as a fast bowler, but could not bowl much because of injury and finished up batting at number three and topping the county averages. He has come a long way since then and is now the mainstay of the South African side with his middle-order batting, fast-medium bowling and brilliant slip fielding. He keeps the batting game simple with a quite orthodox technique; he is a very strong guy and quick to pull and hook whenever he is given the opportunity. His bowling looks fairly innocuous although he has the knack of picking up important wickets. He can also bowl tight spells and put together a string of maidens, which is just what the captain wants to give his quicker bowlers a breather. Altogether an exceptional talent.

Another all-rounder who gives his country great value with his ability to open both the batting and the bowling is India's Manoj Prabhakar but my sixth choice has to be WASIM AKRAM, the explosive Pakistani who, in short spells, can be as quick as any bowler around and is quite capable of changing the course of a game with his mid-to-late-order batting. Like his partner, Waqar Younis, he is not always at his most comfortable when he is bowling with the new ball. However, his ability to make the old one swing quite alarmingly at times more than compensates for that. He has a short, Sunday League-style run-up like Richard Hadlee, although his rather open-chested action is nothing like as classical. As a result, he regularly suffers from groin trouble through wrenching the muscles inside the upper thigh as he tries to extract extra pace. He can still be viciously quick, however, and he is always happy to bowl plenty of bouncers whether he is playing Test or one-day cricket. I suppose his batting has been a bit of a disappointment overall, but he has played some crucial innings, most notably at Lord's in 1992. He is at his most effective when he is taking the attack to the bowlers, although at Lord's he played with great responsibility to nurse his side to a two-wicket victory. It demonstrated his nous as a cricketer, which I would have thought should make him an ideal captain. Like most of his fellow-countrymen, however, he has had his run-ins with the Pakistan authorities. More surprisingly, he did not have the backing of the other players in his first spell as captain and he was quickly sent back to the ranks, although he got another opportunity when they ran into even greater problems with Salim Malik.

1980–9

1   Sir Richard Hadlee

2   Kapil Dev

3   Imran Khan

4   Ravi Shastri

5   Lance Cairns

6   Wasim Raja

RICHARD HADLEE, KAPIL DEV and IMRAN KHAN were at the height of their powers in this period, but there were still a few more all-rounders worthy of our consideration. RAVI SHASTRI probably owed his entry into the Indian side at the age of nineteen to the fact that he was one of Sunil Gavaskar's golden boys from Bombay, but justified his inclusion by taking six wickets on his Test debut in New Zealand and going on to compile an imposing record of 3,830 runs (35.79) and 151 wickets (40.96). As a left-arm spinner, he had a hard act to follow in Bishen Bedi and inevitably suffered by comparison. He made up for his shortcomings with the ball by working so hard at his batting that he transformed himself from a tail-ender into a Test match opener. He was a tall, upright player who was always difficult to dislodge when he was thrusting his big front foot down the pitch. He developed his strokes to such an extent that in 1984–5 he became only the second player, after Sir Garfield Sobers, to hit six sixes in an over in a first-class match.

LANCE CAIRNS also hit his fair share of sixes in his time, but it was his remarkable inswing bowling which brought him his greatest successes, particularly against England. He had only a short run and a strange, open-chested action but he was an immensely strong man and he could be extremely effective when conditions were to his liking. They were very much to his liking at

Headingley in 1983 when he took seven wickets in our first innings and ten in the match to give New Zealand their first Test win in England. He took another seven against us at Wellington in 1983–4 and then helped Jeremy Coney to save the match in a ninth wicket stand of 118, a New Zealand record. It was an uncharacteristic effort by Lance, a very likeable character who usually batted with a smile on his face and liked nothing better than blasting the bowlers around.

England never saw the best of Pakistan's WASIM RAJA, although I put him ahead of other all-rounders of his time like India's Mohinder Amarnath (man of the match in the 1983 World Cup Final) and the West Indies' Roger Harper, whose fielding was the only world-class part of his game. Wasim, an adventurous left-hand batsman and useful leg-spin bowler, did make a century against us at Faisalabad in 1983–4, but success eluded him on his two tours of England. He could play, though, as he showed in the Caribbean in 1976–7 when he averaged 54 against an attack containing Roberts, Croft and Garner.

\*        \*        ●        \*        \*

1970–9

1    Mike Procter

2    Sir Garfield Sobers

3    Eddie Barlow

4    Mushtaq Mohammad

5    Asif Iqbal

6    Bernard Julien

Shane Warne – it has been a privilege to see him bowl.

*Top:* Anil Kumble (left) and Bishen Bedi, two Indian wizards with different ways of getting batsmen out.

*Bottom:* Alan Knott. Was there ever a better wicketkeeper?

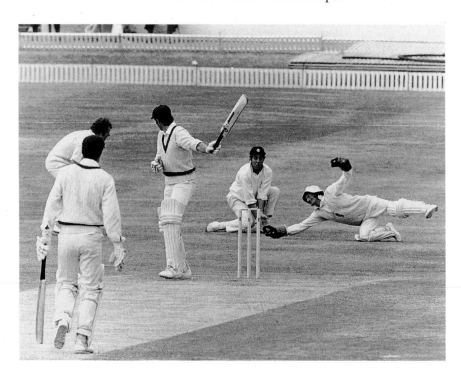

*Top:* We did not call Derek Underwood (left) 'Deadly' for nothing but Phil Tufnell's match-winning performances have been few and far between.

*Bottom:* Jack Russell at his best in South Africa in 1995–6.

Imran Khan, a dominant figure.

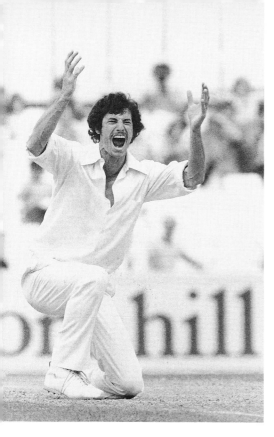
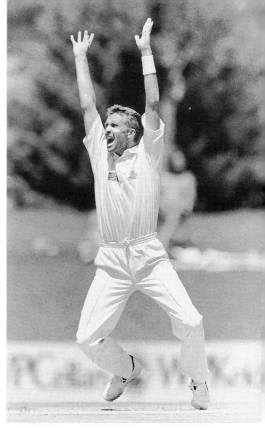

*Top:* Two all-rounders of appeal – Sir Richard Hadlee (left) and
Dominic Cork.
*Bottom:* Sir Garfield Sobers, the greatest all-round cricketer of them all.

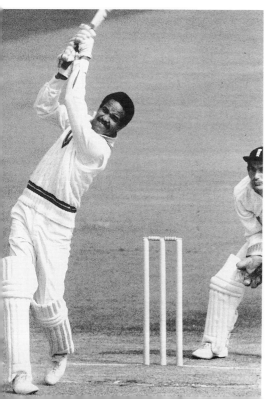

*Top:* Two of cricket's most influential captains, Ray Illingworth (left) and Clive Lloyd.

*Bottom:* Three England skippers, Graham Gooch, Mike Atherton and Mike Gatting.

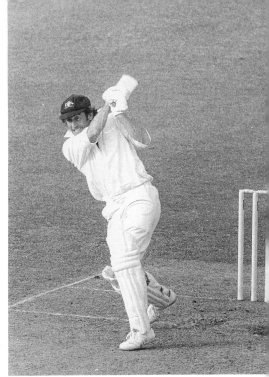

*Top:* Tony Greig (left) and Ian Chappell, captains I enjoyed playing for and against.

*Bottom:* Mike Brearley knew how to get the best out of Ian Botham.

England's top two umpires – David Shepherd and Dickie Bird.

GARY SOBERS – or Sir Garfield as he was by then – was approaching the end of his phenomenal career by the start of this decade, but he was still a sight to behold. I had just had my first look at him in a match between Nottinghamshire and Surrey at Trent Bridge where he came in with the score on 12 for 4, R. G. D. Willis having taken all four wickets. He hit the first ball he faced from me straight back over my head for four and went on to make 104 in an hour and twenty minutes. I had been put well and truly in my place although I could console myself with the fact that I was not the first to suffer at the hands of the great man. He was only twenty-one when he made the then Test record score of 365 not out against Pakistan in Kingston, Jamaica, in 1957 and one can only wonder how many he might have scored if it had not been for a pitch invasion, similar, I suppose, to that which enveloped Brian Lara when he passed the magic figure in Antigua in 1994. Play was abandoned for the day with about an hour to go and Gerry Alexander, the West Indies captain, subsequently declared. But for that, Sobers could well have gone on beyond 400 and given Mr Lara an even bigger target to face. It was just one of many incredible batting performances as he averaged a staggering 57.78 in Test cricket although what many considered to be his greatest innings was not in a Test match at all. It came in 1971–2 when he scored 254 for the Rest of the World against Australia at Melbourne and even Sir Donald Bradman said that he had never seen a better exhibition. There was another remarkable performance at Lord's in 1973 when he scored his twenty-sixth and last Test century despite a severe stomach upset which forced him to go off for a natural break, as they say, in the middle of his innings.

Yet batting was only part of the Sobers story. Apart from his wonderful left-hand batting, he had three different types of bowling at his disposal – genuinely fast left arm, slow left-arm orthodox spin and 'chinamen' out of the back of the hand. He was at his best bowling in his quicker style and Geoffrey Boycott for one would testify to the devastating late swing he could achieve. It was the classic skill of the left-arm fast bowler slanting the ball across the right-hander and then swinging it back into their pads as they covered up their stumps. Finally this most complete of all cricketers was a quite magnificent all-round fielder, a great mover in the outfield before his knees gave out and a spectacular catcher close to the wicket. The only criticism ever aimed at Sobers was over his captaincy, particularly when he declared against Colin Cowdrey's side in Trinidad in 1967–8 and allowed England to win the series, but it is grossly unfair that a great player like him should be remembered for one error of judgment. Not that Gary would consider it an error of judgment at all. Like Ian Chappell, one of Australia's finest captains, he preferred to have a game of cricket than get involved in tedious, boring draws. It epitomises the man when you see him now in the bar of the Pickwick Pavilion at the Kensington Oval in Barbados, enjoying a beer with the members after close of play. No one can ever say that Gary has forgotten his roots or where he learned his unrivalled skills. He is a true ambassador for the game of cricket and it was entirely proper that he should be knighted by the Queen on his native island. The fact that he received the accolade in the middle of the racecourse at the Garrison Savannah made it even more appropriate.

Compared with Sobers's colossal career, MIKE PROCTER's brief spell in Test match cricket was no more than a blip because of South Africa's isolation, but there is no doubt in my mind that he was the outstanding all-rounder of the 'seventies. He played in only seven Test matches, all of them against Australia, and although he absolutely devastated them in 1969–70 with 27 wickets at 13.57 apiece, you have to look at his first-class record to see what an incredible cricketer he really was. He finished with 21,904 runs, including forty-eight centuries, at 36.15, took 1,407 wickets at 19.37 and held 324 catches – and those figures give no indication of his inspirational captaincy which led to Gloucestershire being dubbed 'Proctershire' when he was leading them between 1977 and 1981. A magnificent physical specimen, Procter began his run from close to the boundary edge and accelerated into an amazing whirlwind action which enabled him to swing the ball in late at high pace. His accuracy was such that he did the hat-trick three times in County Championship matches and once in a Benson & Hedges Cup game and he had no qualms about bowling plenty of bouncers either. His Test batting average of 25 does scant justice to his ability but you have to remember that he did not get much opportunity in the South African line-up of the time. He got even less when he played for the Rest of the World against England in 1970, having to go in at number ten, such was the array of batting talent in that side. In fact he was a high-class batsman who scored more than 1,000 runs in a season nine times and, in South Africa in 1970–1, six centuries in successive innings.

One of the reasons why Procter found himself batting so low in the order for both South Africa and the Rest of the World was the presence of EDDIE BARLOW, otherwise known as 'Bunter' because of his glasses and ample frame. They disguised a highly competitive cricketer who was unique in his ability to open both the batting and the bowling until Manoj Prabhakar came along. Although he usually got on as second or third change, he was a very handy new-ball bowler. He was not the most accurate but he bowled at a lively medium pace and was always likely to pick up a wicket or two with his bouncy style and ability to make the ball swing. In fact he picked up four in five balls, including a hat-trick, against England at Headingley in 1970. He was also a very competent opening batsman who was good enough to average over 45 in Test matches despite having to live in the shadow of Barry Richards. As a captain, he had an inspirational effect on Derbyshire in the mid-'seventies, but he did not have such a happy time when he tried to do the same as manager with Gloucestershire.

Another all-rounder good enough to get into that Rest of the World side in 1970 was MUSHTAQ MOHAMMAD, who had become the youngest player in Test match history when he made his debut for Pakistan against the West Indies in 1959 at the age of fifteen. Cricket was very much in Mushtaq's blood, his brothers, Hanif, Sadiq and Wazir, and his nephew, Shoaib, all playing Test cricket, and he was a naturally gifted player. Like most of the Pakistani batsmen of his generation – and they had so much talent that they should have had a lot more success than they did – he was a brilliant player in his home conditions although he was sometimes found wanting on wickets more helpful to seam bowlers. He was particularly good against spin and was one of the first exponents of the reverse sweep. Assessing leg-spinners has become a difficult art since the emergence of Shane Warne, and although Mushtaq had a pretty impressive Test record – 79 wickets at 29 – I never thought he had the control to be considered in the highest class. He had a well-disguised googly and was a formidable proposition in county cricket, where he played for Northamptonshire for many years, although he was not as good as his fellow countryman, Intikhab Alam.

ASIF IQBAL actually opened the bowling on his Test debut for Pakistan against Australia in 1964, but he was very much a batsman who could bowl a bit. Despite not being particularly strong, he was an excellent timer of the ball and an exceptional runner between the wickets. Indeed I think he more than anyone revolutionised that aspect of the game when he was playing one-day cricket for Kent. I would not be surprised if some of Bob Woolmer's skill at getting the best out of his players in a team environment came from playing with Asif. He certainly introduced the same brand of running between the wickets when he was coaching Warwickshire. Asif has since done very well for himself in organising the international tournaments in Sharjah and is obviously as astute off the field as he was on it.

Having started this section with Gary Sobers it is a shade ironic that I should finish it with BERNARD JULIEN, since he had the misfortune to be compared with the incomparable during the early stages of his career. He was certainly in the Sobers mould as a left-arm quick bowler, in that he had the ability to swing the ball into the right-hander and get it to cut away off the seam towards the slip catchers. He was a brilliant strokeplayer as well, as he showed when he was putting us to the sword with a magnificent 121 at Lord's, but I think he got found out by Lillee and Thomson in Australia in 1975–6. He was never quite the same after that. I will never forget my first encounter with him in a second-eleven match for Surrey against Kent. I bowled him a bouncer and, as he shaped to hook, shouted: 'That's out!'

To which Bernard replied: 'Yes – out of the ground.' And, sure enough, it was.

\*       \*       ●       \*       \*

1970–95

1    Sir Richard Hadlee

2    Kapil Dev

3    Imran Khan

4    Mike Procter

5    Wasim Akram

6    Sir Garfield Sobers

## All-time

1     Sir Garfield Sobers

2     Sir Richard Hadlee

3     Kapil Dev

4     Imran Khan

5     Mike Procter

6     Keith Miller

I have already told you what I thought of the first five. My final choice was between Australia's two greatest all-rounders, KEITH MILLER and Richie Benaud, and I think Keith's record – 2,958 runs at 36.97 and 170 wickets at 22.97 – speaks for itself. So does his reputation.

# 9

# WICKETKEEPERS

## England

1990–5

1   Jack Russell

2   Alec Stewart

3   Steve Rhodes

4   Keith Piper

5   Colin Metson

6   Richard Blakey

When I first saw JACK RUSSELL keeping wicket for Gloucestershire in the early 'eighties I thought he was going to be another Alan Knott and, in many ways, I guess he is. There could never be another Knott, of course, because he was quite simply the best all-round wicketkeeper England have ever had, yet there are great similarities between Russell and the man who has become his guru. Not the least of them is his total dedication to the job, which has enabled him to come back from a spell in the wilderness when he must have feared that his Test match career was over. He was not the first England wicketkeeper to lose his place because the selectors wanted to strengthen the batting when they turned to Alec Stewart but his keeping was also being called into question when they preferred Steve Rhodes for the home series against South Africa in 1994 and the winter tour of Australia. It was typical of Russell that he did not sit and sulk but went back to his county and turned himself into a better all-round cricketer. He got back into the side against the West Indies in 1995, averaged nearly 50 in his three Tests, and then went from strength to strength in South Africa, breaking the world record with eleven catches in Johannesburg and scoring many invaluable runs. He has always had a very good pair of hands, particularly standing back where he does not miss very much at all, and is quick to get up to the stumps, which makes the fielding look very neat and tidy and lifts the rest of the team. He is also a great help to his captain in keeping him informed about the line the bowlers are bowling and how they are performing, and at the end of an over he finds time to jog down the pitch and offer a consoling word to a bowler who might have been unlucky. His own problems have come standing up to the spinners – always the acid test of any wicketkeeper – and he has missed some important stumpings.

It looked as though STEVE RHODES was going to keep Russell out for a long time when he first got into the England side and made such an impressive start that at the end of the South African series the captain, Mike Atherton, named him as his player of the year. He had taken twenty-six catches, made two stumpings and averaged 55.50 in his first six Tests but he went sadly off the rails in Australia the following winter when he just did not look the part with either gloves or bat. He missed some straightforward chances in the Tests, both standing up to the stumps and standing back, and never looked like making runs. He seems to be much more at home in one-day international cricket where he is left on his own behind the stumps to dive around to his heart's content.

With Rhodes so quickly found wanting, the selectors reverted to ALEC STEWART, who has yo-yoed his way up and down England's batting order depending on whether he is keeping wicket or not. He is a very reluctant gloveman because he feels that the extra responsibility affects his batting, and the statistics bear this out, but he is willing to do it as long as it keeps him in the side. In fact he has usually kept wicket very well. He has missed the odd chance but he has taken some brilliant catches, including one sensational effort to dismiss Brian Lara at Lord's in 1995 before he broke a finger for the third time in a year at Edgbaston. He is not so comfortable standing up to the spinners – not many wicketkeepers are these days – but he has rarely let England down when he has been asked to do the job.

Stewart certainly has a better pair of hands than either Rhodes or RICHARD BLAKEY who had a desperate time when he was picked along with Stewart for the ill-fated tour of India and Sri

Lanka in 1992–3. It was a badly selected squad which was always going to struggle, although it surprised me how poorly Blakey performed, more so with the bat than with the gloves. He had started his career as a specialist batsman and occasional wicket-keeper; however, as his 'keeping has improved his batting has deteriorated. He kept very competently for Yorkshire in 1995 but averaged only 17 in first-class cricket and with his batting in such decline his name will not be very high on the selectors' list.

The new heir apparent is KEITH PIPER, the Warwickshire wicketkeeper, who has given a very good account of himself on the last two England A tours. He spends a lot of his time standing back to the likes of Allan Donald and Tim Munton although he is also very useful standing up and has had a lot to do with the development of Neil Smith as an off-spin bowler.

Lancashire's Warren Hegg and Leicestershire's Paul Nixon have also featured on recent A tours but my sixth choice is Glamorgan's COLIN METSON who has been very unlucky not to get any international recognition. It can only be because he is not much of a batsman.

\*      \*      ●      \*      \*

1980–9

1   Bob Taylor

2   Alan Knott

3   Jack Russell

4   Bruce French

5   Paul Downton

6   Jack Richards

I was lucky to play nearly all my Test match cricket with either ALAN KNOTT or BOB TAYLOR behind the stumps and I find it hard to believe that there was ever a better wicketkeeper than Knott and very few superior to his faithful deputy and eventual successor. I remember Alan being absolutely devastated after missing a stumping on the 1970–1 tour of Australia and Ray Illingworth coming out with the immortal words: 'At least we know you're ******* human, Knotty!' That just about said it all. Knott was brilliant standing up to the spinners and fantastic standing back to the quicker bowlers. And that is not to mention his batting which was quite outrageous at times. His record speaks for itself. He holds the England wicketkeeping record with 269 dismissals – 250 catches and 19 stumpings – and scored 4,389 runs, including five centuries, at an average of 32.75. He had his idiosyncracies, like the turned-up collar, the handkerchief hanging out of his pocket and a habit of touching the bails when he was batting, and I suppose he was a bit of a hypochondriac, especially on tour. He would go to great lengths to prevent his muscles from stiffening up, which explained all those strange-looking exercises, and he spent a fair amount of time with the physiotherapist, but he was always ready to go out and play. Indeed he was quite nonplussed when he was left out of the side at the end of that 1970–1 tour to give the loyal, uncomplaining Taylor the chance to make his Test debut against New Zealand. Such was the strength of New Zealand cricket in those days that England felt they did not need to play all their front-line players, but Knotty was not very impressed because it broke his long sequence of consecutive appearances.

It was only when Knott went off to play for Kerry Packer in 1977–8 that Taylor got the opportunity to become an England regular and prove that while he may not have been in the same class at a batsman there was not much between them as wicketkeepers. Most of their contemporaries would agree that Knott was a shade better but Taylor probably had the edge when it came to standing up to the stumps. He was often left out of the one-day international side – and, in the end, the Test side as well – to make way for a better batsman yet he played some dogged innings for England, notably at Adelaide in 1978–9 when he made 97 in a stand of 135 with his Derbyshire colleague, Geoff Miller. Above all he was a craftsman and like all good craftsmen he took great care of the tools of his trade. It is interesting, therefore, to hear him talk about modern wicketkeeping gloves and the size of the piece of webbing between the thumb and forefinger. He reckons it is making gloves more like baseball mitts so that wicketkeepers are not catching the ball in the palm of the hand but in the webbing. Needless to say, he is not in favour of it. If you inspected his gloves, you would have found there was hardly any webbing there at all. He was the model professional, taking great pride in his appearance as a representative of his country both on and off the field. His undying devotion to duty at the many cocktail parties we used to have to attend earned him the nickname 'Chat' and his gift of the gab has since served him well in a public relations role with the Test sponsors, Cornhill Insurance.

The first of the batting wicketkeepers to take Taylor's Test place in the desperate search for runs from the lower order was David Bairstow, but after scoring 59 on his debut against India at The Oval in 1979 he did not make another fifty and was soon discarded. The talkative Yorkshireman did not miss much standing back but he was never up to the task standing up. He did better in the one-day internationals which suited his competitive instincts.

Bairstow was replaced in the Test side by PAUL DOWNTON whose potential had been spotted by John Murray, the former Middlesex and England wicketkeeper and then a selector, while he was still understudying Alan Knott at Kent. I think the selectors thought that he would make more runs for England than he actually did but despite some courageous performances – most notably when he opened the batting against the West Indies at Edgbaston in 1984 after Andy Lloyd had been injured, and scored 56 – he finished with the modest average of 19. He was a good-looking wicketkeeper who went on to have a distinguished career with Middlesex before an eye injury caused by a flying bail hastened his retirement.

He was followed into the England team by BRUCE FRENCH who was a classical wicketkeeper in the Bob Taylor mould without ever being quite in the same class. He did not have much luck, either. He was bitten by a dog when he was out jogging on the 1985–6 tour of the West Indies, concussed when he was hit by a bouncer from his Nottinghamshire colleague Richard Hadlee against New Zealand at Lord's in 1986 and developed an infection after being hit in the chest in Australia in 1986–7.

JACK RICHARDS was not as good a wicketkeeper as French but he forced him out of the England side on the 1986–7 tour of Australia on the strength of his superior batting and more than justified his selection with a brilliant century in the second Test at Perth. He also had a good match at Melbourne where England made sure they kept the Ashes. He rapidly became disillusioned, however, when he was picked for only three more Tests in the next two years and retired from the game after his Surrey benefit in 1988.

\*          \*          ●          \*          \*

1970–9

1    Alan Knott

2    Bob Taylor

3    David Bairstow

4    Ian Gould

5    Roger Tolchard

6    Geoff Humpage

England never had to look much further than Alan Knott and Bob Taylor in this period and when they did it was towards wicket-keepers who could bat rather than specialists behind the stumps. I have already mentioned DAVID BAIRSTOW. ROGER TOLCHARD went on a couple of tours as Knott's deputy but he had to wait until his second one to India in 1976–7 to play in a Test match and then it was as a batsman. He did a great job in that role, batting for five and a half hours to make a crucial 67 in our win at Calcutta.

IAN GOULD was another pugnacious batsman, whom I selected for the 1982–3 tour of Australia as well as the 1983 World Cup, and although he did a reasonable job in a one-day context I always get a wry smile from Bob Taylor when we recall him dropping an important catch against New Zealand at Edgbaston.

GEOFF HUMPAGE also played one-day cricket for England after some high scoring and consistent wicketkeeping for Warwickshire but he was never really up to international standard.

1970–95

1   Alan Knott
2   Bob Taylor
3   Jack Russell
4   Bruce French
5   Alec Stewart
6   Paul Downton

\*      \*      ●      \*      \*

All-time

1   Alan Knott
2   Godfrey Evans
3   Bob Taylor
4   John Murray
5   Les Ames
6   Jim Parks

ALAN KNOTT and BOB TAYLOR are joined by GODFREY EVANS and LES AMES, two more legendary wicketkeeper-batsmen from Kent, JOHN MURRAY, who held the world record for most dismissals in a career until Taylor broke it, and JIM PARKS, who got into the England side as a batsman and became the first-choice 'keeper.

*     *     ●     *     *

## Rest of the World

1990–5

1    Ian Healy

2    Jeff Dujon

3    David Richardson

4    Adam Parore

5    Kieron More

6    Andy Flower

One of the main reasons for Australia's domination of Test cricket in recent years has been their foresight in identifying talented young players at an early age and allowing them to develop into world-class performers. IAN HEALY is a prime example of this. He had played only six first-class matches for Queensland when he was picked for the 1988–9 tour of Pakistan and, not surprisingly, he struggled a bit with the uneven bounce and turn. But they kept faith with him and were richly rewarded as he rapidly established himself as the best all-round wicketkeeper in the world. A hard-working cricketer, he keeps himself very fit and is able to maintain his concentration throughout the longest, hottest days. He also scores vital runs, invariably batting positively even when he goes in at 50 for 5. He has always been an excellent wicketkeeper standing back to the quick bowlers, and he had to learn the art of standing up with the emergence of Shane Warne and Tim May as important figures in the Australian attack.

Keeping wicket to the spinners was not something which taxed JEFF DUJON too often, although he did it competently enough when he had to and the West Indies could certainly not have asked for anyone much better to take those flying edges from the fast men. Lithe and acrobatic, he clung to 267 catches in his eighty-one Test matches as well as scoring more than 3,000 runs. They say you never miss someone until they have gone and just how important he was to the West Indian machine has been shown by the way they have struggled to replace him.

DAVID RICHARDSON has been a fixture in the South African side since their return to Test cricket in 1991–2 and it was a shame that he broke a finger in the one-day internationals against England in 1996 and had to miss the World Cup. He has not only kept wicket consistently well but he has also scored vital runs when their notoriously brittle batting has fallen apart. Nearly all his work behind the stumps has been done standing back because of South Africa's seam-orientated attack – in fact his first 100 dismissals in Test cricket did not include a stumping – and he found it much more difficult when the new spin sensation, Paul Adams, was introduced to the side. Standing up is a vital part of the job but it is very difficult to practise it if there are no spinners around.

India's KIERON MORE could have no complaints on that score and while he was not in the same class as predecessors like Farokh Engineer and Syed Kirmani he made a good fist of 'keeping to their array of spinners.

I liked the look of ADAM PARORE when he replaced the injured Ian Smith on New Zealand's tour of England in 1990 and he confirmed that good impression four years later when he not only kept well but also batted with some style, especially at Old Trafford when his 71 helped to save the match.

Like Parore, Zimbabwe's ANDY FLOWER will find it difficult to shine in a struggling side, but he is a talented player and has a key role to play as captain, batsman and wicketkeeper as Zimbabwe strive to establish themselves in international cricket.

1980–9

1    Rodney Marsh

2    Syed Kirmani

3    Jeff Dujon

4    Ian Healy

5    Wasim Bari

6    Ian Smith

It is ironic that when RODNEY MARSH first appeared against us in 1970–1, the discerning Australian public christened him 'Iron Gloves' because he kept dropping the ball. 'Iron Man' would have been more appropriate for one of the greatest of all cricketers who went on to claim a record 355 dismissals in Test matches, score 3,633 Test runs and break the beer-drinking record on a flight from Australia to England. I remember seeing his bruised and battered hands when he was diving all over the place to take the thunder-bolts of Lillee and Thomson during the 1974–5 tour and marvelling at his commitment. He would always go for catches even if they were on their way to first or second slip and he would invariably come up with the ball. He was a great socialiser, who also got himself very fit, training with Lillee at the WACA ground at Perth until they dropped, and was still going strong at the end of the hottest day. He was a ferocious batsman and although he struggled standing up to the stumps at the start of his career, he became very competent there as well. He is now in charge of Australia's famous cricket academy at Adelaide and the youngsters could not have a better example.

It would be hard to find a more contrasting character than SYED KIRMANI, the Indian wicketkeeper who shaved his head for reli-gious reasons, but I rated him second only to Marsh during this period. He had to serve a long apprenticeship under Farokh Engineer, and when he did get into the Test side against New Zealand in 1975–6 he equalled the Test record of six dismissals in an innings in only his second match. He was in his element standing up, having spent most of his early years 'keeping to slow bowlers, and with the emergence of Kapil Dev he turned himself into a terrific all-round wicketkeeper. It was fascinating to see him playing in the World Masters Series in 1995. He was forty-six by then but had lost none of his skills and made some quite brilliant stumpings.

WASIM BARI, whose 228 dismissals put him fourth in the all-time list (behind Marsh, Dujon and Knott), was another high-class wicketkeeper. He had to keep to all kinds of bowling during his fifteen years behind the stumps for Pakistan – off-spinners, leg-spinners, left-arm spinners and, of course, the pace of Imran Khan and Sarfraz Nawaz – and was always thoroughly reliable. He also did his stint as captain of his country – which all the leading Pakistani players seem to have to do – and was a tremendous orchestrator of the chorus from the bat-pad fielders.

New Zealand's IAN SMITH was another wicketkeeper with plenty to say for himself and he was in full voice when he was claiming a lot of victims off Richard Hadlee's bowling in the 'eighties. He was a very competent 'keeper and no mean batsman, either, as I found out to my cost in 1983–4 when his 113 not out at Auckland prevented us from saving the series.

1970–9

1    Rodney Marsh

2    Syed Kirmani

3    Wasim Bari

4    Farokh Engineer

5    Deryck Murray

6    Ken Wadsworth

When it came to appealing, FAROKH ENGINEER was in a class of his own. In fact he turned the whole art of wicketkeeping into something of a stage performance. 'Rooky', as they called him at Old Trafford where he became a great favourite with the Lancashire crowd, was a pretty good gloveman for all that, and, in his prime, a brilliant, forcing opening batsman who once scored 94 before lunch against a West Indies attack containing Hall, Griffith, Sobers and Gibbs.

Much less demonstrative than Engineer but almost as effective was DERYCK MURRAY who played a lot of cricket in England for Cambridge University, Nottinghamshire and Warwickshire as well as appearing in sixty-two Test matches for the West Indies. He took nearly as much punishment from the fast bowlers as Rodney Marsh had done but he stood up to it pretty well. He was prone to the odd mistake but he could always make up for it with the bat. He was a good player to have going in at number seven, good enough in fact to open for the West Indies for a while.

There was not much to choose between KEN WADSWORTH and Warren Lees, who took over from him in the New Zealand side, but I go for Wadsworth because he had to spend a fair amount of time standing up to the left-arm spin of Hedley Howath and was still improving when he tragically died of cancer at the age of twenty-nine.

1970–95

1   Rodney Marsh

2   Ian Healy

3   Jeff Dujon

4   Syed Kirmani

5   Wasim Bari

6   Deryck Murray

All-time

As above. Just as the fast bowlers reached new heights between 1970 and 1995, so, I believe, did the world's wicketkeepers. Two Australians and two West Indians reflect their sides' dominance of Test cricket for much of the period while the skills of an Indian and a Pakistani standing up to the spinners as well as back to the quicker bowlers earn them their places.

# 10

# FIELDERS

## England

1990–5

1 Graeme Hick

2 Phillip DeFreitas

3 Chris Lewis

4 Mark Ramprakash

5 Nasser Hussain

6 Graham Thorpe

It is taking GRAEME HICK a long time to convince the cricket world that he is a genuine Test match batsman, although there has never been much doubt about the quality of his fielding. He is not only a very good outfielder with a strong arm but he is a top-class slip catcher as well. It was completely out of character when he suddenly appeared vulnerable in the West Indies in 1993–4, putting down a number of slip catches, particularly off the left-handers. 'Catches win matches' is one of cricket's oldest clichés, which is true for all that, and the two he put down from Shivnarine Chanderpaul in the Trinidad Test were important misses for which England had to pay a heavy price.

You do not often see PHILLIP DeFREITAS in catching positions close to the bat, but it is unlikely that he would miss much because he is a brilliant fielder everywhere else. He is very quick across the ground with a good, flat throw, a safe catcher and he has become quite an expert at running batsmen out from inside the fielding circle in one-day matches.

The one area of CHRIS LEWIS's game which has served England consistently well in recent times has been his fielding, especially in the gully area where he shows great anticipation. I have already mentioned his athleticism in the all-rounders' section, and his movement around the field allied to a safe pair of hands and a swift pick-up and throw lifts the standard of England's out-cricket every time he is in the side.

MARK RAMPRAKASH made an instant impression with his fielding on his Test debut against the West Indies at Headingley in 1991, diving spectacularly to his right to catch Phil Simmons in the covers and then throwing down the stumps to run out Carl Hooper at the bowler's end. He is not quite as quick across the turf as Lewis but he is panther-like in the covers, has a good pair of hands and a decent arm. He is less reliable close to the wicket.

NASSER HUSSAIN has also contributed brilliantly in the field for England although his appearances have been few and far between and we have seen a lot more of GRAHAM THORPE who has been used as a specialist slip fielder since he got into the side. He has held some good catches but he has dropped a few fairly straightforward ones as well and a success rate of little over fifty per cent suggests that he is not in the same class as some of his predecessors.

*     *     ●     *     *

1980–9

1    Ian Botham

2    Derek Randall

3    Phillip DeFreitas

4    David Gower

5    Chris Old

6    Mike Hendrick

As you would expect, IAN BOTHAM was just as competitive in the field as he was with bat and ball and I have no hesitation in naming him as the outstanding England fielder of my time. His reflexes in the slips, where he took most of his 120 Test catches, were quite remarkable and he was just as brilliant fielding to his own bowling or, on the rare occasions when he got away from the bat, in the outfield. Needless to say, he had a mighty arm from the deep and he was very good at hitting the stumps from anywhere.

I was fortunate enough to be bowling for England at the same time as DEREK RANDALL was turning cover fielding into a performance all of its own. There has never been a fielder quite like 'Arkle' – so called because he never stopped running. He used to walk in a long way (around twenty metres, I guess) before taking up his actual fielding position just as the bowler was delivering the ball and he was already on the move when the batsman played it. He was very fast across the ground with a low centre of gravity, swooping on the ball and, as often as not, hitting the stumps. His throwing was incredibly accurate and he was responsible for some amazing run-outs, none more spectacular than that at Headingley in 1977 when Rick McCosker backed up a shade too far and Randall had his stumps down in a flash.

With Randall on one side of the wicket and DAVID GOWER on the other, there was a period when batsmen playing against England were scared to take the easiest-looking single if the ball was played anywhere near either cover or midwicket. In his younger days, David was very speedy with a quick, underarm throw and it was sad to see his fielding go into such rapid decline when he developed a problem with his right shoulder. It left him with no power in his arm and I always thought that he should have concentrated on turning himself into a good, specialist slip fielder. It did not happen and he was never a particularly good catcher close to the wicket.

Cricket lovers with long memories will remember CHRIS OLD putting down a couple of catches in the nail-biting tension of the 1981 Headingley Test, although they were not typical of a brilliant all-round fielder. He was not only good in the outfield with his safe hands and powerful throw but he did not miss much close to the wicket, either.

MIKE HENDRICK was another of the rare breed of seam bowlers who could field exceptionally well close to the wicket. He was very safe in the slips, where he was particularly adept at diving forward to take the most difficult of all slip catches.

1970–9

1    Ian Botham

2    Derek Randall

3    David Gower

4    Tony Greig

5    Graham Roope

6    Graham Barlow

Like Ian Botham, TONY GREIG was a cricketer who was forever imposing his personality on the game and, like Botham, he could do it just as spectacularly in the field as he could with bat or ball. His most famous bit of fielding, I suppose, was in Trinidad when he ran out Alvin Kallicharran after the last ball of the day had been bowled. There were plenty of other occasions when he had the crowd on its feet, fielding either in the deep, where he had a great arm and held some very good catches, or in the slips, where he took some which were quite amazing for such a tall man.

Less surprising, perhaps, were the acrobatic efforts of GRAHAM ROOPE, who was a goalkeeper with various amateur and part-time professional football clubs and showed what a fine pair of hands he had by taking thirty-five catches in his twenty-one Test matches.

There were some good outfielders around in this period as well, among them John Lever and John Emburey, who could throw a cricket ball harder than most, but my final choice has to be GRAHAM BARLOW. He was a brilliant mover either in the covers or at midwicket until he was crippled by back trouble, and, with Derek Randall, helped to raise the standard of England's fielding in the 'seventies.

1970–95

1 Ian Botham
2 Derek Randall
3 Graeme Hick
4 Tony Greig
5 Graham Roope
6 Phillip DeFreitas

\*     \*     ●     \*     \*

All-time

1 Ian Botham
2 Phil Sharpe
3 Derek Randall
4 Walter Hammond
5 Tony Lock
6 Brian Close

IAN BOTHAM tops this list because he was a brilliant fielder anywhere while the others were specialists – PHIL SHARPE and WALLY HAMMOND incredible catchers in the slips, TONY LOCK and BRIAN CLOSE fearless at short leg and DEREK RANDALL incomparable in the covers.

\*        \*        ●        \*        \*

## Rest of the World

1990–5

1    Mark Waugh

2    Jonty Rhodes

3    Mark Taylor

4    Brian Lara

5    Michael Slater

6    Keith Arthurton

JONTY RHODES is living proof of how rewarding it can be for a young cricketer to work at his fielding. He is a gutsy but limited batsman and I doubt if he would have featured very much at all in the South African side if it had not been for his specialist skills in the covers. He works at his fielding – and you only have to look at the MCC Masterclass video to see how hard he does work at it – in much the same way as the legendary Springbok, Colin Bland, who was reckoned to save his side fifty runs a match. Rhodes is a brilliant mover, very athletic and acrobatic with great anticipation, and no one who saw it will ever forget his run-out of Pakistan's Inzamam-ul-Haq at Brisbane during the 1992 World Cup. He was off the ground parallel to the turf as he demolished the stumps in what was a phenomenal piece of television as well as a phenomenal piece of cricket.

You may be surprised that I have not got Jonty Rhodes at the top of my list, but he is very much a specialist and, for my money, MARK WAUGH of Australia was the best all-round fielder in the world in the first half of the 'nineties. He is almost infallible at second or third slip where he makes the job look easy, and he is quite brilliant away from the bat as well. His ability to hit the stumps seemingly at will is quite extraordinary.

Almost his equal as a world-class slip fielder is his captain, the gum-chewing MARK TAYLOR, who has tremendous powers of concentration and catches most things that come his way from Craig McDermott, Shane Warne or anyone in between. He is a big man – they don't call him 'Tubby' for nothing – and since he is never going to be as mobile in the outfield as some of his more athletic colleagues he has made slip catching into something of an art form. His opening partner, MICHAEL SLATER, is also a good close catcher as well as being very fast in the outfield.

Slip fielding is one area where the West Indies are nothing like as good as they were in the days of Clive Lloyd, Viv Richards and Gordon Greenidge in the 'seventies and 'eighties. There is much less discipline in their approach to the game, with some differences of opinion about how they should be preparing for a day's cricket, and I think it shows in their work in the field. They do have some excellent fielders, including BRIAN LARA, who showed what he could do by running out Graham Thorpe with a ninety-metre throw in the Texaco Trophy match at the Foster's Oval in 1995. He is very quick with a strong and accurate throw for such a small man, although I do not put him in the highest category at slip where he probably drops as many as thirty-five per cent of the chances which come his way.

KEITH ARTHURTON is another great mover who always gives the impression that he is patrolling the covers very well, but again there is a flaw in the West Indian façade. Watch him closely and you will see that he rarely picks the ball up cleanly and even more rarely hits the stumps.

1980–9

1    Viv Richards

2    Roger Harper

3    Gus Logie

4    Allan Border

5    Greg Chappell

6    Javed Miandad

From the moment we saw VIV RICHARDS in the first World Cup Final at Lord's in 1975 we knew that we were watching one of the outstanding fielders of modern times. Five of the Australian batsmen were run out, three of them by Richards, who showed his uncanny ability to hit the stumps by throwing them down from side-on to get rid of Alan Turner and Greg Chappell. He never lost the knack, and he became just as expert in the slips where he took so many catches off the fastest bowlers the world has seen.

It is just as well that ROGER HARPER was such a magnificent fielder because neither his batting nor his bowling were good enough to keep him in or around the West Indies team for such a long time. Superbly athletic in the outfield and quite breathtaking close to the bat, he took some stunning catches, including one in front of the Mound Stand at Lord's to dismiss Ian Botham in the 1984 Texaco Trophy match which almost brought the house down.

Great fielders come in all shapes and sizes and there could hardly have been a more contrasting figure to Harper than the scampering GUS LOGIE. He stands only 5ft 4in but he was amazingly quick across the ground and had no trouble getting the ball in with great accuracy. He was also very good under the helmet at short leg where he had to be quite fearless considering the speed at which the ball sometimes came off the bat against those fast bowlers.

ALLAN BORDER is another little fellow who was a brilliant all-round fielder and ended his career with a record 156 catches in Test cricket. He could not run like Logie and he did not have the most powerful arm, either, but anywhere close to the wicket there have been few better at catching the ball or saving runs than he was. I can remember him taking some fantastic, full-length, one-handed catches in the slips, and apart from that he made the short midwicket position his own. It was a spin-off from the one-day game in which two fielders have to be within fifteen yards of the bat in the first fifteen overs of the innings. I think Border was the first captain to experiment with it in Test matches and he used it to great effect. Ask Graham Gooch!

Before Border, GREG CHAPPELL was Australia's 'Mr Reliable' in the slips where he had that priceless gift which all the great fielders have, of being able to switch his concentration off after each delivery and then turn it back on again the moment the next one was about to be bowled.

There have been few great batsmen who have not been good fielders as well and Pakistan have had none better than JAVED MIANDAD who was brilliantly swift in the covers in his younger days and became an expert slip catcher as he slowed down.

\*　　\*　　●　　\*　　\*

1970–9

1   Viv Richards

2   Greg Chappell

3   Clive Lloyd

4   Ian Chappell

5   Eknath Solkar

6   Bob Simpson

With those thick, heavy glasses of his and that stooping gait, you would never have expected CLIVE LLOYD to be one of the great fielders of all time, but he was – whether it was in the covers in his early days or in the slips, where he set the standard for all the West Indies' close catchers. At the start of his career, his speed about the field was quite sensational and his long arms would come out like telescopes to scoop the ball up and hurl it in. Later on, he moved into the slips where he used his huge mitts and enormous reach to swallow up just about everything that came his way.

The Australian slip cordon in the 'seventies was a remarkable unit with IAN CHAPPELL, his brother Greg, Doug Walters, Rick McCosker and Ashley Mallett ready to pounce on the numerous edges induced by Lillee, Thomson and company, and there were plenty of offerings for the Indian close catchers when their great spinners were in their pomp. One of them was Yajuvindra Singh who actually equalled the world record of seven catches in the first of his three Tests against us in 1976–7, but the best I saw was EKNATH SOLKAR who was both agile and fearless at short leg.

You do not have to look any further than their coach, BOB SIMPSON, to see who taught the present crop of Australian close fielders the art of slip catching. 'Simmo' had established a reputation as one of the finest slippers the world has seen when he retired from Test cricket in 1968 and he had lost little of his expertise when he returned ten years later to help to rebuild a side which had been decimated by the Packer revolution.

*     *     ●     *     *

1970–95

1     Viv Richards

2     Mark Waugh

3     Clive Lloyd

4     Greg Chappell

5     Roger Harper

6     Mark Taylor

All-time

1   Viv Richards

2   Mark Waugh

3   Colin Bland

4   Bob Simpson

5   Clive Lloyd

6   Neil Harvey

Close to the bat or away from it, CLIVE LLOYD, VIV RICHARDS and MARK WAUGH have set the standard for today's generation of cricketers. The other three were legends – BOB SIMPSON at slip and COLIN BLAND and NEIL HARVEY in the covers.

# 11

# MOST HUMOROUS MOMENTS

### 1: Piggies in the Middle

The funniest incident I have seen on a cricket field was at Brisbane during a one-day international when a pig bearing the names Eddie (Hemmings) and Botham on its back was released on the outfield. The prank was played by two medical students who anaesthetised the piglet, put it in their ice box and bore it to the ground. They had stuck an apple in its mouth so that when the contents of their 'eskie' were inspected at the turnstiles it would look as though they were going to have it for lunch. As the morning wore on the anaesthetic wore off and they let it go to poke fun at our two heavyweights.

### 2: Wot No Bat?

I had plenty of fun poked at me at Edgbaston in 1982 when I went out to continue my innings after the tea interval against Pakistan without my bat. It was a strange thing to happen, really, because a bat was the only piece of batting equipment I had. I used to borrow the rest of the gear from the other players, usually Ian Botham if he was out. On that occasion, he said that I could borrow his batting gloves as long as I wore the inner gloves as well. I had so much else on my mind (I was captain at the time) that the message must have gone to my brain that once I had put on the inner gloves I was ready to go. I just tucked the batting gloves under my arm thinking that they were my bat and strode off to the middle. It was only when I got there and prepared to face Imran Khan that I realised I didn't have it with me.

### 3: X Marks the Spot

Mike Gatting must have struggled to see the funny side of it when he got back to England to have his nose rebuilt after Malcolm Marshall had smashed it in Jamaica in 1986, but it gave the rest of us a smile. On arrival at the airport, a reporter asked him: 'Where exactly did it hit you, Mike?' Apart from the fact that he looked like Chi-Chi with his two black eyes, there were two huge pieces of sticking plaster criss-crossing the spot where his nose had been.

## 4: Who Needs a Runner?

Australian wicketkeeper Ian Healy brought the house down at Trent Bridge in 1989 when he added insult to injury in scoring a rapid 29 not out to enable his side to tie a one-day international. When he started limping, England allowed him to have the fleet-footed Dean Jones to run for him. They were not as amused as the crowd when he clipped the ball away and ran two, keeping pace with his runner all the way. England appealed and Jones was sent off.

## 5: Dickie's Hot Line

Umpire Dickie Bird is a bag of nerves at the best of times but Ian Botham and Allan Lamb almost reduced him to a gibbering wreck with their practical jokes. One of their better ones was when Lamby marched in to bat during a Test match and handed Dickie his mobile phone. After a while, it rang. 'Ian Botham here,' said Beefy. 'Tell that bloke Lamb to get on with it.' Another time they laid a trail of firecrackers in his path so that when he walked in from square leg they exploded under his feet. To Dickie's credit, he took it all in good part and even used it to his advantage. His trials at the hands of Beefy and Lamby form the bulk of his after-dinner speeches.

## 6: After You, Skipper

When we arrived in Pakistan in 1977–8, we had a briefing from the British High Commission about the possibility of political activity at the cricket grounds and Mike Brearley lectured us about what we should do if there was any trouble. His instructions were that we should congregate in the middle, stick together and make no attempt to leave the field. Sure enough, a demonstration began during the first Test at Lahore whereupon the police began firing off tear gas, which instead of dispersing the activists blew straight across the ground. Coughing and spluttering, ten of us gathered in the centre of the pitch as per our instructions only to see the back of our gallant captain disappearing in the direction of the dressing room.

# 12

# CAPTAINS

---

1970–95

England

1    Mike Brearley

2    Ray Illingworth

3    Tony Greig

4    Bob Willis

5    Mike Atherton

6    David Gower

England have played under eighteen captains since I made my Test debut in Australia in 1970–1, and before I assess them all in chronological order I think it is worthwhile examining their respective records.

|  | Tests | Won | Lost | Drawn |
|---|---|---|---|---|
| Ray Illingworth* | 25 | 8 | 5 | 12 |
| Tony Lewis | 8 | 1 | 2 | 5 |
| Mike Denness | 19 | 6 | 5 | 8 |
| John Edrich | 1 | 0 | 1 | 0 |
| Tony Greig | 14 | 3 | 5 | 6 |
| Mike Brearley | 31 | 18 | 4 | 9 |
| Geoff Boycott | 4 | 1 | 1 | 2 |
| Ian Botham | 12 | 0 | 4 | 8 |
| Keith Fletcher | 7 | 1 | 1 | 5 |
| Bob Willis | 18 | 7 | 5 | 6 |
| David Gower | 32 | 5 | 18 | 9 |
| Mike Gatting | 23 | 2 | 5 | 16 |
| John Emburey | 2 | 0 | 2 | 0 |
| Chris Cowdrey | 1 | 0 | 1 | 0 |
| Graham Gooch | 34 | 10 | 12 | 12 |
| Allan Lamb | 3 | 0 | 3 | 0 |
| Alec Stewart | 2 | 0 | 2 | 0 |
| Mike Atherton** | 28 | 7 | 10 | 11 |

*Illingworth captained England in six Tests in 1969, winning four and drawing two.
**Atherton captained England in one Test in January 1996, which was lost.

Top six in terms of percentage wins

| Brearley | 58% (18 wins in 31 Tests) |
|---|---|
| Willis | 39% (7 wins in 18 Tests) |
| Illingworth | 32% (8 wins in 25 Tests) |
| Denness | 32% (6 wins in 19 Tests) |
| Gooch | 29% (10 wins in 34 tests) |
| Atherton | 25% (7 wins in 28 Tests) |

Others who captained England ten times or more

| Greig | 21% (3 wins in 14 Tests) |
|---|---|
| Gower | 16% (5 wins in 32 Tests) |
| Gatting | 9% (2 wins in 23 Tests) |
| Botham | 0% (0 wins in 12 Tests) |

RAYMOND ILLINGWORTH was my first England captain and a major influence on my career. It was just like a fairytale when I was plucked out of obscurity in the winter of 1970–1 to fly out to Australia and play with the likes of Boycott, Edrich, Cowdrey, Knott, Snow and Illingworth himself, and he was very kind and considerate towards me. The Australians were still playing eight-ball overs in those days and since I was only twenty-one and not very strong he did not ask me to bowl long spells. Quite apart from that, he also taught me a lot about the game of cricket. He was almost thirty-six when he took over the captaincy in 1969 and he was a shrewd tactician and excellent under pressure. He had a poor relationship with his manager and vice-captain on my first tour (Kent's David Clark and Colin Cowdrey) but he won back the Ashes after twelve years and earned the enormous respect of the Australians. He believed in playing a balanced side – our team in Australia had Illy himself batting at number six, Alan Knott at seven and four bowlers from eight to eleven – but he has not found it an easy thing to do becoming England's first supremo in 1995. He declined to tour India and Pakistan in 1972–3 and was sacked from the captaincy after losing the 1973 series against the West Indies.

In Illingworth's absence, TONY LEWIS was the establishment appointment for the tour of India and Pakistan, and though he scored 70 not out at Delhi and 125 at Kanpur, he was not a good enough player to represent England when all the top batsmen were available, and he played in only one more Test against New Zealand.

MIKE DENNESS took over from Illingworth for the 1973–4 West Indies tour and although he was not a particularly strong character he was a great competitor. Ironically, it was two of his rivals for the job, Tony Greig and Geoff Boycott, who saved his skin by winning the Trinidad Test and levelling the series 1–1, and he was still in charge for the trip to Australia the following winter. Apart from being ill for much of the tour, he had no chance against Lillee and Thomson and actually dropped himself for the Sydney Test. He returned for the last Test at Melbourne and with Lillee and Thomson injured scored 188 and won the match. They were soon back to haunt him, though, and he was sacked after losing the first Test against Australia at Edgbaston in 1975.

JOHN EDRICH, not a natural captain, took over for the Test Denness missed in Australia. He lost the match and with it the Ashes but he batted with great courage, finishing with 33 not out in the second innings after Lillee had broken two of his ribs with the first ball he faced.

TONY GREIG, who succeeded Denness in 1975, was the second

England captain to make a great impact on me. I had run out of
steam in the Centenary Test at Melbourne in 1977 and he sat me
down and talked to me about the importance of fitness to a fast
bowler. He told me to look at the way Dennis Lillee had kept going
in that match and said that I was going to have to do a lot more
work on my fitness. His words struck home and I went into a very
strict training schedule when I got home. It was the springboard to
the most successful period of my career. Greig suffered badly with
epilepsy and had to sleep every afternoon when he was not on the
field, but he had learned his cricket the hard way in South Africa
and he had a very tough attitude to the game. He was an inspira-
tion to any side and his leadership was seen at its best in India in
1976–7 when he won the first three Tests to take the series. It was
a great loss to English cricket when he joined Kerry Packer and Ian
Chappell in plotting the revolution which led to the formation of
World Series Cricket.

With Greig gone, England looked to his vice-captain, MIKE
BREARLEY, and what an inspired choice he turned out to be. He
was lucky in that he never had to captain the side against the West
Indies, but his record against everyone else speaks for itself. His
first task was to integrate the Packer players into the England team
of 1977 and he did that so successfully that we regained the Ashes,
but perhaps his greatest achievement was in getting the best out of
Ian Botham. He was an excellent man manager (Philippe Henri
Edmonds was his only failure) with a keen desire to win, and he
gained Botham's respect at a very early stage. He led England to a
5–1 victory in Australia in 1978–9 and although he came down to
earth there the following winter when we lost 3–0, he returned in
triumph in 1981. The only drawback with Brearley was that when
he was in the side we could only have four bowlers; the only criticism that he probably overbowled Botham and precipitated his
back problems.

GEOFF BOYCOTT fulfilled his dream of leading England when
Brearley had his arm broken in a practice match at Karachi in
1977–8, but it turned into a bit of a nightmare. After one drawn
Test in Pakistan, he became the first England captain to lose a Test
match against New Zealand and although he managed to square
the series his one success had as much to do with Botham running
him out and the rest of us persuading him to declare, as his own
powers of leadership.

I think it was Brian Close who persuaded Alec Bedser, then
chairman of the selectors, that IAN BOTHAM was the man to
succeed Brearley, although he was never really suited to the job. He

had a terrific cricket brain and was inspirational once he got on to the field, but the discipline of practice and administration was not his cup of tea. He was also unlucky to meet the West Indies in most of his Tests as captain and it was a harrowing experience for him when his manager, the much-loved Kenny Barrington, died in Barbados in 1981.

KEITH FLETCHER had a tremendous reputation in county cricket. He got off on the wrong foot as England captain, though, by complaining about the umpires early in his tour of India in 1981–2 and never got out of his head the thought that they were biased. Then he followed India's captain, Sunil Gavaskar, down the path of slow over rates which led to one of the most boring series of all time. He and the manager, Raman Subba Row, also had enormous problems with Geoff Boycott, who eventually went home, while other players became disillusioned and signed up for the 'rebel' tour of South Africa.

This meant that Fletcher's successor, one BOB WILLIS, had to captain England with fifteen of the best players banned for going to South Africa. It was a tough job as the leading fast bowler in the side and I also found it very hard work dealing with the Press, but it was very satisfying to beat a strong Pakistan side in 1982. Criticisms? Well, I did not think that I handled Ian Botham well on tour and I just could not fathom P. Edmonds, who should certainly have gone on the 1982–3 Australian tour. Like Brearley, I was lucky not to captain England against the West Indies.

DAVID GOWER was not so fortunate. He had stood in for me against Pakistan at Lord's in 1982 and at Faisalabad and Karachi in 1983–4 before taking over in his own right against the West Indies in 1984. He lost that series 5–0 and was to lose 5–0 again in the Caribbean in 1985–6. He also lost the Ashes in 1989, but he had had his moments, leading England to a very creditable victory in India in 1984–5 and winning the Ashes the following summer. Before he became captain, he did not think much about selection or other players' problems, so they came as a bit of a shock to him; yet, for all the relaxed style, he did think very deeply about the job. He clashed early on with Graham Gooch, never really hitting it off with him, and his captaincy was further undermined by the South African plotters and defectors in 1989. In common with all England captains after Mike Brearley, he had precious little bowling at his disposal.

Gower suffered from his 'laid-back' label and was probably a better captain than the not-so-laid-back MIKE GATTING whose reign should have been finished by his run-in with umpire Shakoor

Rana in Pakistan in 1987–8, rather than by the ridiculous barmaid affair the following summer. It is quite amazing that although he will be remembered for retaining the Ashes in 1986–7, his two victories on that tour were the only Tests he won. Highly regarded on the county circuit, he had a tough one-eyed approach to captaincy. He was not scared to admonish players on the field and would probably have got more out of Phil Tufnell than his other skippers have done. He was also a good political player with the establishment. Some of them even wanted him back as captain after he had led the last 'rebel' tour to South Africa.

Gatting's removal led to two bizarre appointments – JOHN EMBUREY, who had a couple of losing Tests against the West Indies but would not even have been picked for the next one at Headingley because no spinner was required, and CHRIS COWDREY who took over for that one Test and has since earned a decent living speaking after dinner about his exploits. He was a crazy selection because he was never worth his place. He was subsequently fined for writing in the Press about his exclusion.

GRAHAM GOOCH did initially put some pride back into England's performances, but his pedantic attitude towards fitness and practice did not suit all individuals. He certainly led by example, playing some of his best innings while he was captain, but he was not good at handling different types of superstar. He should clearly have included Gower more often, but Gower just was not a Gooch clone. He did well in successive series against the West Indies, losing only 2–1 in the Caribbean and holding them 2–2 at home, but the selection for the 1992–3 tour of India was a terrible mish-mash with too many one-day specialists being picked to play in a Test series. No one remembers one-day results unless it is the World Cup.

ALLAN LAMB had a pretty thankless task, standing in for Gooch in three Tests (one in Australia, two in the West Indies), and ALEC STEWART fared no better, presiding over England's first defeat by Sri Lanka and losing in India when Gooch was ill.

The selectors were right to prefer MICHAEL ATHERTON when Gooch finally threw in the towel. He made plenty of mistakes in the field early on and he was fortunate to survive the 'dust in the pocket' incident against South Africa at Lord's in 1994, but he has the makings of a good captain. He has not had much to work with. His own form has stood up very well although his batsmen have consistently let him down and he has never had a settled bowling attack. He is a tough character with the right attitude to the opposition; however, like all England's recent captains, he will continue to struggle until the 'Willis Blueprint' for cricket is adopted and the county game becomes more competitive.

\*　　　\*　　　●　　　\*　　　\*

## Rest of the World

1　Ian Chappell

2　Clive Lloyd

3　Imran Khan

4　Greg Chappell

5　Allan Border

6　Geoff Howarth

IAN CHAPPELL's performance in leading Australia to a 2–0 win over the West Indies in the Caribbean in 1973 was one of the outstanding achievements in modern cricket. He had lost Dennis Lillee, who had sustained a very serious back injury, and Bob Massie, whose bowling had gone to pieces after his incredible performance in England, but even with people like Max Walker, Jeff Hammond, Doug Walters and a couple of spinners to do the bowling, he beat Rohan Kanhai and company convincingly. Ian was a captain who really did know how to mould a team and get the best out of it. He was a terrific motivator who thought a lot about his players and told them how good they were and he always played unselfishly himself to try to get them into winning positions. Although he was blessed with Lillee and Thomson for some of the time, there were plenty of other occasions when he had to rely on the medium pacers and spinners to win him Test matches. He was a tough character but a sporting opponent who always tried to have a game of cricket. He was not very keen on scores of 500 or 600;

he much preferred playing in Test matches where the scores were around 250 or 300 because they made for better contests.

GREG CHAPPELL led Australia in a slightly different style to Ian and tarnished his reputation somewhat when he instructed their younger brother, Trevor, to bowl underarm to prevent the New Zealand batsmen hitting a six off the last ball to win an international match. I think we can dismiss that as an aberration caused by the pressures of the game and the expectations of a one-day crowd, showing that these things tell on even the hardest characters. Greg was very uncompromising on the field and I remember him admonishing Rodney Marsh for telling the umpire, Tom Brooks, that a 'catch' off Derek Randall had not carried during the Centenary Test, although I don't think you could say that either of the Chappells would bend the rules to their own advantage. They very much wanted to win, but they wanted to win fair and square.

I guess CLIVE LLOYD was responsible for making Test cricket the game it is today. Having been thrashed in Australia by a side including Lillee, Thomson, Walker and Gilmour and then beaten by India in Trinidad with a team containing three spinners, he persuaded Clyde Walcott, then chairman of the West Indies selectors, that fast bowlers would always take wickets quicker than spinners under any conditions. The four-man pace attack was born, and while it is a moot point whether Clive did cricket a service or a disservice, we certainly saw some fantastic fast bowling in the ensuing years. It did not take any great powers of leadership to rotate the quicks, hour after hour, day after day, to make sure that there were always two of them fit and ready to fire but there was more to Lloyd than that. He relished the responsibility of captaincy, scoring fourteen of his nineteen Test centuries while he was in charge, and uniting the islands in a way that only the legendary Sir Frank Worrell had been able to do. Viv Richards certainly found him a hard act to follow, and although the West Indies carried on winning, there were times when Richards seemed to be just a little bit too keen to maintain their dominance.

IMRAN KHAN never let up in his efforts to inspire Pakistan to the kind of results their talents warranted, and when Wasim Akram and Waqar Younis came along he finally got his reward. Pakistan at last had a pace attack to be reckoned with, and for a while he welded together the different factions in Pakistan cricket and got everyone pulling in the same direction. His crowning glory was the World Cup triumph in Australia in 1992 and it told you everything about his influence when he retired and the team began to fall apart again. It is no easy task to achieve harmony and unity in such a political climate as we saw in 1995, when they had four different captains in Wasim Akram, Salim Malik, Moin Khan and Ramiz Raja.

ALLAN BORDER experienced the extremes of emotion in his record ninety-three Tests as Australia's captain. He was sometimes in despair when he was leading a losing side in his early days, but they were forgotten when he returned home with the Ashes to ticker-tape welcomes in 1989 and 1993. Border deserved the acclaim because he had stuck with it when lesser men would have admitted defeat. They called him 'Captain Grumpy', but anyone would have been grumpy with the limited resources he sometimes had to work with and he lifted Australia out of the doldrums as much by personal example as anything else.

GEOFF HOWARTH was the most successful captain New Zealand have ever had, leading them to eleven victories in his thirty Tests in charge. He was fortunate to have Richard Hadlee in his side and perhaps even more fortunate to have the New Zealand umpires around as well, but to lead them to victory against the all-conquering West Indians in 1980 was no mean feat. He also masterminded New Zealand's first win in England in 1983 and their first success in a series against us in 1983–4.

# 13

# UMPIRES

## England

1  David Shepherd

2  Dickie Bird

3  Charlie Elliott

4  Barrie Meyer

5  Alan Whitehead

6  Peter Willey

I believe that we should look at umpires in the same way as we do players and remember them when they were at their best, so although he is not quite as good as he was a couple of years ago I make DAVID SHEPHERD England's top umpire of recent times. The Test and County Cricket Board certainly seem to think so since he has been England's representative at the last two World Cups and I think they have got it just about right. I played a bit of cricket against 'Shep' when he was a hard-hitting middle-order batsman with Gloucestershire and one of the most popular figures in the game, and he has lost little of his popularity since taking up umpiring in 1981. It took him only four years to get on to the Test match panel and he was one of the first umpires to be appointed when the National Grid International Panel was set up in 1994. He is best known for his superstition of the dreaded 'Nelson' which always sees him hopping about with one foot off the ground, but I don't think he would hesitate to give a batsman out even if he was on 111.

DICKIE BIRD's decline was reflected by the fact that he finally lost his place on the international panel in 1996, but you do not stand in a record sixty-five Test matches without being a very fine umpire and, arguably, the best the game has seen. It was entirely appropriate that the TCCB should give him one more Test against India at Lord's so that he could go out at the top. He is still on the first-class list where he has been since 1969, and that in itself is a measure of his consistency. I spent some time on the TCCB committee responsible for selecting umpires and I can assure you that their marks are constantly under scrutiny. My only criticism of Dickie is that he was and probably still is a 'not outer'. Most captains – the men who do the marking – are batsmen and I think umpires who tend to be 'not outers' are always going to get higher marks than umpires like Ken Palmer, who is more likely to give people out on close calls. In his prime, Dickie had the enviable reputation of getting most things right, but he lost a bit of credibility when he called for the 'third umpire' watching the television replay to make the decision when Graeme Hick was run out in the Texaco Trophy match against the West Indies at the Foster's Oval in 1995. You have to remember that if the TV cameras had not been able to provide a decent replay Hick would not have been given out when in fact he was clearly run out by about four yards.

When I was captaining England, one of my fellow selectors was CHARLIE ELLIOTT who, I believe, is the only umpire, certainly in recent times, to go on and become a Test selector. He was still umpiring at the start of my career and I found him to be very conscientious. He was not afraid of the controversial moments out in the middle and his reputation for impartiality was so great that he was even invited to stand in one of our Test matches in New Zealand in 1970–1. He was just as conscientious as a selector. Picking Test teams is an inexact science but Charlie was very good at expressing his opinions about players without fear or favour. I think that umpires could be consulted more about who does and does not play well, particularly in pressure-cooker situations.

BARRIE MEYER lost his place on the Test match panel a few years ago, but I always enjoyed playing when he was umpiring. He made a number of quite obvious mistakes in Test matches, and he was a big enough character to own up to them. I can remember a couple of occasions during my time as England captain when he came up to me and said: 'Sorry, Bob, I got it wrong.' I believe that it is vitally important for umpires to admit their mistakes because such honesty gives the players as much confidence in them as all the good decisions they make. An umpire who has thought about what he has done, maybe looked at the television highlights programme in the evening and then been prepared to admit that he got it wrong deserves the utmost respect.

Of the many other English umpires who have come and gone over the years, Don Oslear got a few players' backs up through being too officious and the same can be said of ALAN WHITE-HEAD although I think he is still a pretty good umpire. Sometimes his approach is not quite as conciliatory as it might be and he gets a bit over-excited in his confrontations with players in tense situations. Whitehead has always been very strong in dealing with excessive short-pitched bowling and pernickety even over no-balls, although there is nothing wrong with that because it is quite amazing how many no-balls some umpires allow to go unpunished. There was an obvious example of this in the summer of 1995 when Cyril Mitchley, the South African umpire on the international panel, allowed the West Indians to get away with any number of no-balls. There cannot be anything more galling for a batsman than to lose his wicket and then see on the television replay that the bowler was six or eight inches over the front line when he delivered the ball.

I may be jumping the gun a bit with my final choice because, at the time of writing, PETER WILLEY has yet to stand in a Test match, but I do believe that he is going to be a very fine umpire. And I was delighted to see that the TCCB shared my opinion when they appointed both him and his former Northamptonshire colleague, George Sharp, to the international panel in 1996. 'Will' has made an excellent start to his new career, taking all the professionalism and dedication he showed as a batsman against the West Indian fast bowlers into his umpiring. He is a very determined character who will not stand any nonsense from anybody and I expect to see him right at the top of the tree before too long.

## Rest of the World

1    Srinivas Venkataraghavan

2    Douglas Sang Hue

3    Swaroop Kishen

4    David Archer

5    Steve Bucknor

6    Lou Rowan

It is a tough job umpiring in the international arena these days under the constant gaze of the television cameras and it is not surprising that one or two umpires seem to be feeling the pressure, but whenever I have seen SRINIVAS VENKATARAGHAVAN he appears to be completely unfazed by it all. This is the same Venkat who played in fifty-seven Test matches for India, captaining them between 1975 and 1979, as an off-spinner, spent three seasons with Derbyshire and has played hockey, badminton and snooker to a reasonable standard. He has also worked as a sports writer and a radio and television commentator and all that experience seems to have stood him in good stead since he took up umpiring in 1991. He goes about his business in a quiet, calm and authoritative manner and makes very few mistakes.

Although I understand he went off markedly when he did some umpiring in World Series Cricket, I thought that when he was at his best DOUGLAS SANG HUE of the West Indies was one of the finest umpires in the world. Before the National Grid International Panel came into existence, visiting players had the feeling that if any close decisions came along the home side would get the benefit of the doubt. At the same time, England players always felt that the reverse was true when teams visited us because our umpires would bend over backwards to give them the benefit. Be that as it may, I never had any qualms about Sang Hue and I thought he showed what a good umpire he was when he gave Alvin Kallicharran out after Tony Greig had thrown down the stumps as he was setting off for the pavilion at close of play. It was not within his province to say: 'No, Tony, you shouldn't have done that.' He was out there to make a decision and he gave the right decision. The fact that it was later reversed did not alter that.

There have been few finer sights in world cricket over the years than that of SWAROOP KISHEN, the roly-poly Indian umpire, standing there chewing his betel nut and sweating profusely during the long, hot days of a Test match on the subcontinent, but his appearance belied the fact that he was a very good umpire. Visiting teams were not always happy about the umpiring in that part of the world but Swaroop exuded confidence and the players had confidence in him. He got most of the decisions right and that is the important thing as far as they are concerned.

I always enjoyed the company of DAVID ARCHER who, when he was not umpiring, ran a bar at the back of the members' stand at the Kensington Oval in Barbados until his untimely death at an early age. He was a nice guy, a very relaxed character who was always ready to have a drink and a chat at close of play. Like all umpires, he made mistakes and, perhaps because he was from the Caribbean, he was prepared to allow a bit too much short-pitched bowling, but he always seemed to be in control out in the middle and ready to diffuse awkward situations with a quiet word.

STEVE BUCKNOR from Jamaica is not dissimilar to David Archer in the way that he gets quietly on with the job. He has had a couple of shaky series recently but he has won the confidence of cricketers in all the Test-playing countries. He was certainly the best umpire in the World Cup in Australia in 1992 and I am sure he will be on the international panel for a few more years to come. Apart from his umpiring, he is very helpful to the media, letting people know what is going on if there is any disruption due to the weather and keeping them up to date.

Over the years, England had enormous problems with the umpires in Australia, not necessarily because they were biased, although one or two of them were bordering that way, but because we were on the wrong end of some shocking decisions out there. It meant that we did not have too much confidence in them, although LOU ROWAN, a former police officer, was an exception. I think most of our players trusted him although he did fall out with Ray Illingworth and John Snow in a big way on the 1970–1 tour. Lou was always ready to stand his ground and when he came across a character as stubborn as Illingworth he was determined to dig in his heels. Unfortunately he had got it wrong when he warned Snow for hitting Terry Jenner with a ball that was not all that short and provoked so much crowd trouble that Illy took us off the field.

It is because it is absolutely crucial for players to have confidence in the umpiring that the introduction of the National Grid International Panel is one of the best things to have happened in cricket in my time. When an international panel was first mooted, the idea was to have two 'neutral' umpires standing in each Test, but that would have given precious little opportunity for the home umpires to gain the experience they need because they would never have had an opportunity of standing in a home Test. The system of having one visiting member of the panel standing with a home umpire is a good compromise and I congratulate the International Cricket Council on getting it right.

# 14

# COMMENTATORS' BLUNDERS

### 1

I guess the most famous commentators' blunders were those perpetrated by Brian Johnston, although 'Johnners' was such a consummate professional with a great sense of fun that I doubt whether they were blunders at all. Off-the-cuff remarks like 'The bowler's Holding, the batsman's Willey' and 'One ball left' after Pat Pocock had been treated for a blow where it hurts, were probably scripted well in advance and just waiting for the moment to arrive.

### 2

More spontaneous, perhaps, was the episode when 'Johnners' and his fellow commentator, Jonathan Agnew, sent listeners into fits of laughter by going into great detail about how Ian Botham 'didn't quite get his leg over' during the Test match between England and the West Indies at The Oval in 1991.

### 3

My Sky colleague, Charles Colvile, was silenced for once when someone was kind enough to bring us some ice cream when we were commentating on a Test match. Charles was enjoying it so much that he started talking into his cone instead of the microphone.

### 4

John Arlott was almost as famous for his love of wine as he was for his cricket commentaries, and his fondness for quaffing a bottle or two during the day led to the odd embarrassing moment. He was so taken by a Worcestershire batsman whom he took to be Phil Neale during a televised Sunday League game that he started ruminating about why he was not in the England side. After a while there was a long pause before John intoned: 'All is explained . . . this is Imran Khan.'

### 5

John used to share those Sunday League games with Jim Laker who, for fairly obvious reasons, would always do the last session.

He still came on the air too late on one occasion because John actually fell asleep during his own stint. The BBC had a rookie stage manager on duty who was too scared to wake him and they had to make do without any commentary for several minutes.

## 6

Sometimes, of course, you wish you had kept quiet. Early in my broadcasting career, the cameras closed in on the former England manager, M. J. K. Smith, who was sitting on the Edgbaston balcony watching the Test match through his rimless glasses. 'There he is,' I said, 'the bespeckled Mike Smith!'

# 15

# BEST TEAMS

---

## 1970–95

### England

### 1: Ray Illingworth's Team in Australia 1970–1
### Fourth Test at Sydney

Geoff Boycott
Brian Luckhurst
John Edrich
Keith Fletcher
Basil D'Oliveira
Ray Illingworth
Alan Knott
John Snow
Peter Lever
Derek Underwood
Bob Willis

This side has a special meaning for me because it was the one in which I made my Test match debut. It was a dream come true when I got a call in November to pack up my winter coaching job at the Crystal Palace recreation centre and fly out to replace the injured Alan Ward. Until then, I had just pretended to be some of these guys playing cricket in the back garden with my brother, David, and there I was out there with them as part of the team. Australia had held the Ashes for twelve years and England had not been given any serious chance of bringing them home. The scheduled six-Test series had started with two high-scoring draws at Brisbane and Perth, the Gabba seeing a double century by Keith Stackpole and the WACA witnessing the arrival of Greg Chappell who began his Test career with a hundred. After the second match, David Clark, the England manager, was quoted as saying that he would prefer to lose the series by three matches to nil rather than sit through any more boring draws. This got Ray Illingworth's back up and widened the already gaping chasm between the Kent alliance of Clark and Colin Cowdrey, the vice-captain, and the old-fashioned professional Yorkshireman. The third Test at Melbourne was so badly hit by rain that the powers that be, Sir Donald Bradman and Sir George 'Gubby' Allen among them, decided that it would be futile to start a Test after the first three days had been washed out, agreed that we should play a one-day international instead and brought a whole new dimension to international cricket. It was against this background that I was given my debut because of another injury to Ken Shuttleworth.

Since becoming England's cricket supremo, Illingworth has always said that his ideal would be to play a balanced side with at least five bowlers, and you will see that this team gave him the perfect mix. There were three all-rounders (D'Oliveira, Knott and Illy himself) at numbers five, six and seven with Snow batting as high as eight in front of Lever, Underwood and Willis. It just shows the confidence he had in the top four batsmen, and they rarely let him down, with Boycott, Edrich and Luckhurst quite outstanding. This allowed him plenty of variety in the bowling. There was the unique left-arm spin of Underwood, his own off-spin, the seam and swing of D'Oliveira, one high-class fast bowler in Snow, a work-horse quick in Lever and the rookie Willis setting out on his Test career.

Sydney did not offer a very good surface and Snow was the central figure in the match. He had the ability on that tour to bowl what could only be described as a 'throat-ball' length, and most of the Australian batsmen struggled to play against him. Some of the umpires, Lou Rowan in particular, thought that his bowling was intimidatory but he was not actually bowling bouncers. He was pitching only just short of a length but the bounce he was able to achieve off the hard pitches was phenomenal.

*Result: England (332 and 319–5 dec.) beat Australia (236 and 116) by 299 runs.*

## 2: Mike Brearley's Team v. Australia in 1977
## Third Test at Trent Bridge

Mike Brearley
Geoff Boycott
Bob Woolmer
Derek Randall
Tony Greig
Geoff Miller
Alan Knott
Ian Botham
Derek Underwood
Mike Hendrick
Bob Willis

In considering this team, it is important to remember that it was the time of the Packer revolution, which had been hatched during the Centenary Test match at Melbourne in March and revealed to the world when the Australians were playing Sussex at Hove early in the tour. Packer's England players (Greig, Knott, Underwood and Woolmer among them) had initially been threatened with expulsion from the Test team but in the event the only major effect was the removal of Greig from the captaincy, which gave Brearley his first chance to lead England. It was a difficult job for him because Greig had been a high-profile captain who had not only had great success in India the previous winter but also done an excellent public relations job for the game. However, Brearley was in his element. He was a tremendous captain from a psychological point of view and with Australia's will and determination under severe pressure as a result of the Packer shenanigans, he was just the man to exploit the situation. While our Packer men were easily integrated into the side, Greg Chappell, who was no mean captain himself, had a thankless task trying to keep his troops together. Some of them were on the Packer payroll but others had been overlooked and they were a pretty unhappy bunch. Our side also had two notable inclusions – Geoffrey Boycott, who had returned from the wilderness after going into exile following the Old Trafford Test against India in 1974, and Ian Terence Botham, who was making his Test debut at the age of twenty-one.

Boycott began by running out the local hero, Randall, which did not go down too well with the Trent Bridge faithful, but he made up for it with a century, and with Knott also making a characteristic hundred we took control of the game. For his part, Botham managed to persuade Greg Chappell to drag a long hop into his stumps for his first wicket in Test cricket and went on to pick up four more. The rest, as they say, is history.

*Result: England (364 and 189–3) beat Australia (243 and 309) by seven wickets.*

## 3: Tony Greig's Team in India 1976–7
### Third Test at Madras

Dennis Amiss
Bob Woolmer
Mike Brearley
Derek Randall
Roger Tolchard
Tony Greig
Alan Knott
John Lever
Chris Old
Derek Underwood
Bob Willis

I cannot speak too highly of the way Tony Greig galvanized this side into a fine working unit. It was quite extraordinary to find ourselves 3–0 up after three Test matches in India, where nearly every previous England team had struggled through illness, injury and flat pitches on which only the Indian spinners could make any impression. Greig played his trump card early in the tour by getting the home supporters on his side. He would do impressions of the players, India's as well as England's, to humour them and they really took to him. His players took to him, too.

There were several survivors from Ray Illingworth's 1970–1 side in Australia, which gave us a solid base, a fast-emerging young batsman in Randall, who was to finish the tour in triumph at the Centenary Test, and a good, balanced attack. We had Lever with his left-arm swing, Old, who was capable of swing and seam at no mean pace, and myself as the strike bowler. Greig could bowl both medium pace and the off-spin which had been so successful against the West Indies a few years earlier, while the ever-reliable Underwood was still there either to block up an end or take advantage of the conditions if there was any help for him. The batting might have looked stronger if Keith Fletcher had not suffered an ankle injury but Tolchard, nominally the reserve wicketkeeper, played as a specialist batsman and did an excellent job for us. We had won at Delhi, where Lever took ten wickets on his debut and did not deserve to be smeared by the Vaseline business, and at Calcutta, where Greig got up from his sick bed to play one of the great captain's innings. Now this side clinched the series on one of the quickest wickets I have ever seen.

*Result: England (262 and 185–9 dec.) beat India (164 and 83) by 200 runs.*

### 4:  Mike Brearley's Team v. Australia, 1981
### Fourth Test at Edgbaston

Geoff Boycott
Mike Brearley
David Gower
Graham Gooch
Mike Gatting
Peter Willey
Ian Botham
John Emburey
Bob Taylor
Chris Old
Bob Willis

I have gone for the team which won the second of England's three famous victories in 1981 because it had a slightly better balance than the one which hit back to stun Australia at Headingley and then beat them again at Old Trafford. Botham was seriously into his pomp by this stage. He had blown away both New Zealand and Pakistan in 1978 and had another outstanding series against India in 1979. He then ran into problems as captain in back-to-back series against the West Indies, but as soon as he relinquished the job and Brearley took over again he was restored to his former glory. Having inspired the Headingley drama with his 149 not out, he demolished the Australians at Edgbaston by taking five wickets for one run in twenty-eight balls and completed an incredible tour

de force with arguably his finest Test hundred at Old Trafford.
Nobody, not even Botham, could manage to score fifty in the match
in question which ended abruptly when Australia, chasing a fairly
modest target for the second match in succession, again collapsed
under pressure. Botham was obviously the dominant figure in a
series in which the Australian captain, Kim Hughes, made some
bad tactical errors, but even so it was a good team performance by
England. Brearley was still struggling as a batsman but Boycott was
there, and Gooch, Gower, Gatting, Willey and Botham made a
formidable middle-order. We had three proven seamers in Willis,
Old and Botham, augmented by the spin of Emburey and, if
required, Willey.

*Result: England (189 and 219) beat Australia (258 and 121) by
twenty-nine runs.*

5: Mike Gatting's Team in Australia 1986–7
Fourth Test at Melbourne

Chris Broad
Bill Athey
Mike Gatting
Allan Lamb
David Gower
Ian Botham
Jack Richards
Phillip DeFreitas
John Emburey
Phil Edmonds
Gladstone Small

This was the last England team to hold the Ashes. They were
written off at the start of the tour when one cricket correspondent
said the only three things wrong with them were that they could
not bat, bowl or field. They had the last word by winning not just
the Ashes but the America's Cup Challenge and the World Series
Cup as well. The old hands, Botham, Lamb and Gower, found
themselves playing under a new captain in Gatting and a new style
of management from Micky Stewart. There was obviously some
friction between the old and the new and Stewart finally weeded
out one or two of the big names when Gooch took over. They were

all overshadowed on this tour by Broad, who played so consistently well that he carried off the prize for the 'International Cricketer of the Year'. There were other notable contributions from DeFreitas, who looked like developing into a worthwhile England all-rounder, and Richards, who not only kept wicket very well but also scored plenty of runs, including a maiden Test century at Perth. Sadly it turned out to be DeFreitas's best tour and Richards's last – within fifteen months Richards had given up cricket altogether and gone to live in the Netherlands. Small did not get into the side until this match but he lost no time in making an impression on the series. He gave England a brilliant start by taking 5 for 48, and with Botham taking the other five wickets Australia were all out for 141. A Broad century consolidated England's position and the Middlesex spin twins, Edmonds and Emburey, completed the job.

*Result: England (349) beat Australia (141 and 194) by an innings and fourteen runs.*

### 6: David Gower's Team in India 1984–5
### Fourth Test at Madras

Graeme Fowler
Tim Robinson
Mike Gatting
Allan Lamb
David Gower
Chris Cowdrey
Paul Downton
Phil Edmonds
Neil Foster
Pat Pocock
Norman Cowans

It was a fine performance by this combination of high-quality crick-eters and run-of-the-mill county players to win in India after England had again been demoralised by the West Indies at home. Some of them were not going to play a lot of Test cricket but they performed very creditably throughout and, on their day, above their mean ability, to take the series 2–1. Robinson had an outstanding tour, averaging 63 over the five Tests, although it was Fowler and Gatting who put this side on the way to victory with a

double century apiece. Lamb and Gower provided more experience
in the middle order and although Cowdrey did not contribute a
great deal as the all-rounder he certainly enjoyed himself more than
he did on his one appearance as England's captain against the West
Indies. Downton had a good tour with both gloves and bat, and
the wickets were almost equally shared between the two seamers,
Foster and Cowans, and the two spinners, Edmonds and the
veteran Pocock. Eleven of Foster's wickets came in this match as
he revealed the talent which should have brought him much more
success than it did.

*Result: England (652–7 dec. and 35–1) beat India (272 and 412)
by nine wickets.*

# Rest of the World

## 1: Clive Lloyd's West Indians in Australia 1979–80
### Third Test at Adelaide

Gordon Greenidge
Desmond Haynes
Viv Richards
Alvin Kallicharran
Lawrence Rowe
Clive Lloyd
Deryck Murray
Andy Roberts
Joel Garner
Michael Holding
Colin Croft

There cannot have been many sides stronger than this one to take the field in Test cricket. The nuclear warhead assembled by Clive Lloyd was tried and tested by the late 'seventies and this particular combination of fast bowlers was probably the most terrifying that even the West Indies have put together. There was Roberts with his two devilish bouncers (one quick, the other quicker) and vicious away movement, Holding with his lightning pace, Garner with his steep bounce from a good length and Croft with his constant intimidation. If they were not enough to scare the pants off anybody, just look at the batting line-up. Greenidge and Haynes, the best pair of openers of their generation, were followed by Richards, Kallicharran, Rowe and Lloyd, four of the greatest strokemakers of all time, and there was still a wicketkeeper-batsman as good as Murray at number seven. England were in Australia at the same time as them because there were two Test series being played in conjunction with the triangular World Series Cup. Australia beat the best side that we could put out 3–0 but they were simply no match for Lloyd's all-stars. It showed what a gulf there was between us and the West Indies at the time.

*Result: West Indies (328 and 448) beat Australia (203 and 165) by 408 runs.*

2:  Ian Chappell's Australians v. England 1974–5
Fourth Test at Sydney

Ian Redpath
Rick McCosker
Ian Chappell
Greg Chappell
Ross Edwards
Doug Walters
Rodney Marsh
Max Walker
Dennis Lillee
Ashley Mallett
Jeff Thomson

This was the side which regained the Ashes for Australia by giving them a winning 3–0 lead in a demoralising six-Test series which England eventually lost 4–1. Australia had already been good enough to beat us at Brisbane and Perth but now they were strengthened by the inclusion of McCosker to make his debut as Redpath's opening partner. They began with a stand of 96, McCosker going on to make 80, and laid the foundation for a total of 405 in which both the Chappells made half-centuries. Edwards was not in the same class as a batsman but he was a wonderful cover point in an exceptional fielding side and Walters and Marsh made sure there was no lack of depth in the batting. Lillee and Thomson were in their prime, Walker gave our batsmen no respite and Mallett showed his worth as an off-spinner by taking four cheap wickets to finish us off.

*Result: Australia (405 and 289–4 dec.) beat England (295 and 228) by 171 runs.*

3: Viv Richards's West Indians in Australia 1988–9
First Test at Brisbane

Gordon Greenidge
Desmond Haynes
Richie Richardson
Carl Hooper
Viv Richards
Gus Logie
Jeff Dujon
Malcolm Marshall
Curtly Ambrose
Courtney Walsh
Patrick Patterson

Almost ten years on from Lloyd's great side, but this West Indian team showed no signs of weakening. One or two of the elder statesmen had disappeared from the batting line-up to make room for new blood in Richardson, Logie and Hooper. They were not as good as Rowe, Kallicharran and Lloyd but they were no mean Test batsmen. Richardson was in his element when the ball was not moving around too much, Logie always seemed to make runs when the West Indies were in trouble, and although Hooper was already an enigma, his off-spin provided useful variety. In any case, Greenidge, Haynes and Richards were still there and Dujon was an even better wicketkeeper-batsman than Murray had been. Meanwhile a new generation of fast bowlers had emerged, among them Patterson who had bowled some of the quickest deliveries I have ever seen when England were in the Caribbean in 1986. His pace was complemented by the inimitable bowling skills of Marshall, the menace of Ambrose, who had already shown that he could achieve the same steep bounce as Garner but at greater speed, and the persistence of Walsh, who was beginning a phenomenal period in which he was able to bowl and bowl and keep picking up wickets with an old ball that looked like a rag.

*Result: West Indies (394 and 63–1) beat Australia (167 and 289) by nine wickets.*

4:  Allan Border's Australians in England 1993
Second Test at Lord's

Mark Taylor
Michael Slater
David Boon
Mark Waugh
Allan Border
Steve Waugh
Ian Healy
Merv Hughes
Shane Warne
Tim May
Craig McDermott

Border's teams had recovered the Ashes in England in 1989 and held them in Australia in 1990–1 and now they came back with an even stronger side which showed how much better than us they are at planning ahead. Four years earlier, they had dropped Boon to number three to let Taylor open with Geoff Marsh and this time it was Marsh who had to give way so that the amazingly talented Slater could open with Taylor. Between them, they made a magnificent opening pair, Taylor looking as solid as a rock yet scoring just as quickly as his more flamboyant partner. Slater marked his first appearance in a Test match at Lord's with a magnificent 152; Boon, established in his new role, scored 164 not out; Mark Waugh made 99 and Border 77 so that Steve Waugh hardly got a knock. Healy performed remarkably throughout the tour with both gloves and bat, Warne was a revelation and May gave him great support. The strength of the side was demonstrated by the fact that McDermott, the main strike bowler, was taken ill and played no part in the match. The lion-hearted Hughes made sure he was not missed.

*Result: Australia (632–4 dec.) beat England (205 and 365) by an innings and 62 runs.*

5: Imran Khan's Pakistanis v. West Indies 1990–1
First Test at Karachi

Shoaib Mohammad
Ramiz Raja
Zahid Fazal
Javed Miandad
Salim Malik
Imran Khan
Salim Youssuf
Wasim Akram
Mushtaq Ahmed
Abdul Qadir
Waqar Younis

Imran Khan finally got what he wanted – a team strong enough to take on and beat the best in the world. The key was the emergence of the two young fast bowlers, Waqar and Wasim, whose fifteen wickets in this match meant that their great mentor did not even have to take the field in the second innings after receiving a blow on the leg. The attack was completed by two high-class leg spinners, the old master, Qadir, and his apprentice, Mushtaq. Youssuf was a good enough wicketkeeper to take more than a hundred dismissals in Test cricket and there was plenty of batting. Shoaib has had a chequered career as an opening batsman but his Test average of almost 47 is better than that of his father, the legendary Hanif. Miandad made only 23 runs in his two Tests in the series but Malik made up for that with 285, including 102 to set up this satisfying victory.

*Result: Pakistan (345 and 98–2) beat West Indies (261 and 181) by eight wickets.*

6:  Mohammad Azharuddin's Indians v. England 1992–3
Third Test at Bombay

Navjot Sidhu
Manoj Prabhakar
Vinod Kambli
Sachin Tendulkar
Mohammad Azharuddin
Pravin Amre
Kapil Dev
Kieron More
Anil Kumble
Rajesh Chauhan
Venkatapathy Raju

All the traditional strengths of Indian cricket came together in this line-up which made England the first side to lose every Test in a series on the subcontinent. The crucial figure was Prabhakar whose ability to open both the batting and the bowling enabled India to field three spinners as well as five more specialist batsmen and the all-rounder extraordinaire, Kapil Dev. There were some dashing strokeplayers in the middle order, the prodigious Tendulkar, his pal, Kambli, and the gifted Azharuddin whose responsibilities as captain have not affected his batting. On the contrary, they seem to have improved it. Kapil was still chasing the world wicket-taking record and the spinners came in three varieties – the orthodox left arm of Raju, the off-spin of Chauhan and the unique leg-spin of Kumble. They took twelve wickets between them in this match; Prabhakar and Kapil did the rest.

*Result: India (591) beat England (347 and 229) by an innings and fifteen runs.*

# 16

# SPORTING GESTURES

## 1

There have been few more sporting gestures in my time than Gary Sobers's declaration against England in Trinidad in 1968–9 . . . and his reaction after it had cost him the Test match and the series. You can still get an argument in the Caribbean about whether he did the right thing when he set England 215 in 165 minutes and then saw them knock them off with three minutes to spare to win by seven wickets. But Gary has never had any regrets. Ever the gambler, he much preferred to risk everything on winning than play out a boring draw. The game of cricket may have been disserved by the number of captains who have refused to follow his example. I cannot remember a sporting declaration in my career.

## 2

There were few tougher opponents on a cricket field than the great Australian wicketkeeper Rodney Marsh, but he showed what a sportsman he was during the Centenary Test at Melbourne in 1977. Derek Randall, who was teasing and tormenting the Australians on his way to an unforgettable 174, had reached 161 when umpire Tom Brooks gave him out caught behind. Rod immediately indicated that the ball had not carried and Derek was recalled.

## 3

A similar thing happened when Bob Taylor was batting during India's Jubilee Test at Bombay in 1980. Umpire Hanumantha Rao gave him out caught behind although he clearly had not touched the ball and when Bob protested, the Indian captain, Gundappa Viswanath, supported him. Again the umpire was persuaded to change his mind. It was a sporting gesture which cost 'Vishy'. Bob went on to share a stand of 171 with Ian Botham which went a long way towards winning the match.

## 4

I am not sure whether Geoff Cope appreciated the gesture when Mike Brearley showed great sportsmanship in the first Test against Pakistan at Lahore in 1977–8. The England off-spinner thought he had done the hat-trick when he dismissed Abdul Qadir and Sarfraz

Nawaz with successive balls and then had Iqbal Qasim caught by Brearley at first slip. His joy was short-lived as his captain, not sure whether the ball had carried or not, withdrew the appeal.

## 5

New Zealand's captain, Jeremy Coney, could not have been more sporting at Lord's in 1986 after the England wicketkeeper, Bruce French, had been hit on the head by a Richard Hadlee bouncer. With French still groggy, Coney allowed Bob Taylor to abandon his hospitality duties in the Cornhill tent until a replacement, Bobby Parks, arrived.

## 6

That man Marsh again, along with his buddy, Doug Walters, always showed great sportsmanship when England were playing in Australia. They were invariably the first visitors to our dressing room clutching a few cans of the amber nectar at the end of a day's play. In the fierce cauldron of Test cricket, it was good to have characters like them to diffuse the most explosive situation.

# 17

# MOST EXCITING TESTS

## 1: Dunedin, 1979–80

*West Indies won toss. New Zealand beat West Indies by one wicket.*

This dramatic New Zealand victory, only the sixth by a one-wicket margin in the history of the game, made them the only team to beat the West Indies in a series in a nineteen-year period between their thrashing in Australia in 1975–6 and their home defeat, again at the hands of Australia, in 1994–5. The West Indies did not like it. They had arrived in New Zealand claiming to be the best side in the world after winning their first series in Australia at the sixth attempt but found themselves neutered by umpiring which they claimed to be totally incompetent if not downright biased. Clive Lloyd's decision to bat first was a questionable one on a pitch which not only allowed plenty of movement but was also keeping low and it looked as though he had got it wrong when Richard Hadlee took three wickets in his first thirteen balls and went on to finish with 5 for 34. He had shown the West Indies how to bowl, but not for the first time and certainly not the last they made the mistake of bowling far too short so that although they took a tremendous battering New Zealand were able to build a first innings lead of 109 thanks to half-centuries by Bruce Edgar and that man Hadlee. He took another six wickets in the West Indies' second innings (his eleven in the match included a record seven lbws), but Desmond Haynes became the first player to bat throughout both innings of a Test match by adding 105 to his earlier 55, and with support from Collis King and Deryck Murray managed to set New Zealand 104 to win.

Then the fireworks began. The mild-mannered Michael Holding kicked the stumps out of the ground after having an appeal for caught behind against John Parker turned down, and his frustration was complete when he hit Lance Cairns's off stump without dislodging a bail. New Zealand were then 96 for 8 and it was 100 for 9 when last man Steve Boock joined Gary Troup. Boock survived five balls from Holding before Joel Garner began the final over. Boock almost ran himself out trying to take a second bye off the first ball, survived a massive lbw appeal off the second and then edged two runs behind point off the fourth to level the scores. The last ball went off his pads to backward square, Derek Parry threw wildly to the non-striker's end and the batsmen scampered through to complete a famous victory.

### WEST INDIES

| | | | |
|---|---|---|---|
| G. Greenidge c Cairns b Hadlee .... | 2 | – lbw Hadlee ............ | 3 |
| D. Haynes c and b Cairns ......... | 55 | – c Webb b Troup ....... | 105 |
| L. Rowe lbw Hadlee ............ | 1 | – lbw Hadlee ............ | 12 |
| A. Kallicharran lbw Hadlee ........ | 0 | – c Cairns b Troup ....... | 0 |
| C. Lloyd lbw Hadlee ............ | 24 | – c Lees b Hadlee ........ | 5 |
| C. King c Coney b Troup ........ | 14 | – c Boock b Cairns ....... | 41 |
| D. Murray c Edgar b Troup ...... | 6 | – lbw Hadlee ............ | 30 |
| D. Parry b Boock ............. | 17 | – c and b Hadlee ......... | 1 |
| J. Garner c Howarth b Cairns ..... | 0 | – b Hadlee ............. | 2 |
| M. Holding lbw Hadlee .......... | 4 | – c Cairns b Troup ....... | 3 |
| C. Croft not out .............. | 0 | – not out .............. | 1 |
| Extras (lb8, nb9) ............ | 17 | – (lb4, nb5) ............ | 9 |
| Total ................... | 140 | ................... | 212 |

1–3, 2–4, 3–4, 4–72, 5–91, 6–105, 7–124, 8–135, 9–136
1–4, 2–21, 3–24, 4–29, 5–117, 6–180, 7–186, 8–188, 9–209

| | | | | | | | | | |
|---|---|---|---|---|---|---|---|---|---|
| Hadlee | 20 | 9 | 34 | 5 | | 36 | 13 | 68 | 6 |
| Troup | 17 | 6 | 26 | 2 | | 36.4 | 13 | 57 | 3 |
| Cairns | 19.5 | 4 | 32 | 2 | | 25 | 10 | 63 | 1 |
| Boock | 13 | 3 | 31 | 1 | | 11 | 4 | 15 | 0 |

### NEW ZEALAND

| | | | |
|---|---|---|---|
| J. Wright b Holding ............ | 21 | – b Holding ............ | 11 |
| B. Edgar lbw Parry ............. | 65 | – c Greenidge b Holding ... | 6 |
| G. Howarth c Murray b Croft ...... | 33 | – c Greenidge b Croft ..... | 11 |
| J. Parker b Croft .............. | 0 | – c Murray b Garner ...... | 5 |
| P. Webb lbw Parry ............. | 5 | – lbw Garner ........... | 5 |
| J. Coney b Holding ............ | 8 | – lbw Croft ............ | 2 |
| W. Lees run out .............. | 18 | – lbw Garner ........... | 0 |
| R. Hadlee c Lloyd b Garner ....... | 51 | – b Garner ............. | 17 |
| L. Cairns b Croft ............. | 30 | – c Murray b Holding ..... | 19 |
| G. Troup c Greenidge b Croft ..... | 0 | – not out .............. | 7 |
| S. Boock not out ............. | 0 | – not out .............. | 2 |
| Extras (b5, lb2, nb11) ........ | 18 | – (b7, lb5, nb7) ......... | 19 |
| Total .................... | 249 | (9 wickets) ........... | 104 |

1–42, 2–109, 3–110, 4–133, 5–145, 6–159, 7–168, 8–232, 9–236
1–15, 2–28, 3–40, 4–44, 5–44, 6–44, 7–54, 8–73, 9–100

| Holding | 22   | 5 | 50 | 2 | | 16 | 7 | 24 | 3 |
|---------|------|---|----|---|-|----|---|----|---|
| Croft   | 25   | 3 | 64 | 4 | | 11 | 2 | 25 | 2 |
| Garner  | 22.5 | 8 | 51 | 1 | | 23 | 6 | 36 | 4 |
| King    | 1    | 0 | 3  | 0 | |    |   |    |   |
| Parry   | 22   | 6 | 63 | 2 | |    |   |    |   |

## 2: Headingley, 1981

*Australia won toss. England won by eighteen runs.*

This will always be remembered as one of the most remarkable of
all the Test matches played between England and Australia. It was
an extraordinary game of cricket to start an extraordinary sequence
of three matches which made it Ian Botham's summer and Ian
Botham's Ashes. There was no hint of the drama to come after
Mike Brearley, recalled to take over the captaincy from the belea-
guered Botham, lost the toss to Kim Hughes. We did not bowl that
badly but we did not bowl well enough to take the wickets we
should have done as they reached 401 for 9 declared, John Dyson
making 102 and Kim Hughes and Graham Yallop providing solid
support. Then we collapsed against the bowling of Dennis Lillee,
Terry Alderman and Geoff Lawson so that when bad light stopped
play on Saturday night we still needed 222 to make them bat again
with only nine wickets left. It was a subdued England team that
turned up at the regular Botham barbecue at Epworth on South
Humberside, where he lived in those days, with many of us contem-
plating not just the loss of a Test match but the end of our Test
careers.

I had not even been included in the original selection for the
match. I had had flu during the second Test at Lord's and been
unable to perform at my best and when I missed the next county
game for Warwickshire, Alec Bedser, the chairman of selectors,
rang me to say that Brearley was not happy about playing anybody
who was not a hundred per cent. With Brearley himself in the side,
of course, it meant that we could only include four front-line
bowlers so there was obviously no room for any passengers. I
managed to persuade Alec that the only reason I was not playing
for Warwickshire was so that I would be OK for the Test, but he
said that I would have to play in a one-day game for the second
eleven to prove my fitness. He then rang the Derbyshire secretary
and got him to intercept Mike Hendrick's invitation to play at
Headingley. Back at the barbecue, Ian did his best to lift our spirits
but those of us who were getting a bit long in the tooth still thought
that it was the end of the road when we checked out of the hotel

on the Monday morning in the belief that the Test would be over that evening.

There seemed no reason why we should change our minds when our seventh wicket went down at 133 – still a little matter of 157 runs behind – before 'Beefy' changed the course of history with what was not much more than one almighty slog. It was remarkable for two things – one that his shots kept coming off and the other that Hughes never used Ray Bright's left-arm spin against him. Graham Dilley and Chris Old joined in and even our last man, some bloke called Willis, managed to hold out until the close when we were 124 ahead. Unfortunately I could not contribute much more next morning, getting myself caught in the slips off Alderman for 2 and leaving Ian stranded on 149, and it still looked to be Australia's game when they set out to make 130 to win.

Ian did get Graeme Wood out early on, but they were coasting along at 56 for 1 until I changed ends and picked up three quick wickets before lunch. I think that is when we began to win the psychological battle. During the interval, we started to believe that we could actually win the game, while they were thinking that 72 was still a lot to get. They were to lose their last six wickets for 53 and although I managed to pick up most of them there were also crucial contributions from Old, who took the important wicket of Allan Border, and the fielders, who held some outstanding catches. Bob Taylor took two of them, one down the legside, another on the offside; Mike Gatting hung on to two more at short leg and mid-on and Dilley somehow kept his feet inside the boundary rope at long leg to catch Rodney Marsh.

All sorts of records were broken in the match. It was only the second time, and the first this century, that a side had won a Test match after following on; both wicketkeepers broke world records, Marsh for the most dismissals in Tests, Taylor for the most catches in first-class cricket; and my figures of 8 for 43 were the best in a Headingley Test. It will also be remembered for another statistic – the odds of 500–1 Ladbrokes offered against us winning. Lillee and Marsh took advantage, as anyone in their right minds would have done, because you do not often get that kind of price in a two-horse race, but I think the England players were too preoccupied to avail themselves of the bookmakers' generosity. It has never been seen again.

## AUSTRALIA

| | | | |
|---|---|---|---|
| J. Dyson b Dilley | 102 | – c Taylor b Willis | 34 |
| G. Wood lbw Botham | 34 | – c Taylor b Botham | 10 |
| T. Chappell c Taylor b Willey | 27 | – c Taylor b Willis | 8 |
| K. Hughes c and b Botham | 89 | – c Botham b Willis | 0 |
| R. Bright b Dilley | 7 | – b Willis | 19 |
| G. Yallop c Taylor b Botham | 58 | – c Gatting b Willis | 0 |
| A. Border lbw Botham | 8 | – b Old | 0 |
| R. Marsh b Botham | 28 | – c Dilley b Willis | 4 |
| G. Lawson c Taylor b Botham | 13 | – c Taylor b Willis | 1 |
| D. Lillee not out | 3 | – c Gatting b Willis | 17 |
| T. Alderman not out | 0 | – not out | 0 |
| Extras (b4, lb13, w3, nb12) | 32 | – (lb3, w1, nb14) | 18 |
| Total (9 wickets dec.) | 401 | | 111 |

1–55, 2–149, 3–196, 4–220, 5–332, 6–354, 7–357, 8–396, 9–401
1–13, 2–56, 3–58, 4–58, 5–65, 6–68, 7–74, 8–75, 9–110

| | | | | | | | | |
|---|---|---|---|---|---|---|---|---|
| Willis | 30 | 8 | 72 | 0 | 15.1 | 3 | 43 | 8 |
| Old | 43 | 14 | 91 | 0 | 9 | 1 | 21 | 1 |
| Dilley | 27 | 4 | 78 | 2 | 2 | 0 | 11 | 0 |
| Botham | 39.2 | 11 | 95 | 6 | 7 | 3 | 14 | 1 |
| Willey | 13 | 2 | 31 | 1 | 3 | 1 | 4 | 0 |
| Boycott | 3 | 2 | 2 | 0 | | | | |

## ENGLAND

| | | | |
|---|---|---|---|
| G. Gooch lbw Alderman | 2 | – c Alderman b Lillee | 2 |
| G. Boycott b Lawson | 12 | – lbw Alderman | 46 |
| M. Brearley c Marsh b Alderman | 10 | – c Alderman b Lillee | 14 |
| D. Gower c Marsh b Lawson | 24 | – c Border b Alderman | 9 |
| M. Gatting lbw Lillee | 15 | – lbw Alderman | 1 |
| P. Willey b Lawson | 8 | – c Dyson b Lillee | 33 |
| I. Botham c Marsh b Lillee | 50 | – not out | 149 |
| R. Taylor c Marsh b Lillee | 5 | – c Bright b Alderman | 1 |
| G. Dilley c and b Lillee | 13 | – b Alderman | 56 |
| C. Old c Border b Alderman | 0 | – b Lawson | 29 |
| R. Willis not out | 1 | – c Border b Alderman | 2 |
| Extras (b6, lb11, w6, nb11) | 34 | – (b5, lb3, w3, nb5) | 16 |
| Total | 174 | | 356 |

1–12, 2–40, 3–42, 4–84, 5–87, 6–112, 7–148, 8–166, 9–167
1–0, 2–18, 3–37, 4–41, 5–105, 6–133, 7–135, 8–252, 9–319

| | | | | | | | | |
|---|---|---|---|---|---|---|---|---|
| Lillee | 18.5 | 7 | 49 | 4 | 25 | 6 | 94 | 3 |
| Alderman | 19 | 4 | 59 | 3 | 35.3 | 6 | 135 | 6 |
| Lawson | 13 | 3 | 32 | 3 | 23 | 4 | 96 | 1 |
| Bright | | | | | 4 | 0 | 15 | 0 |

## 3: Melbourne, 1982–3

*Australia won toss. England won by three runs.*

The England captain, one R. G. D. Willis, was showing obvious signs of wear and tear by the time we got to Melbourne for the fourth Test of the series. We had drawn the first match in Perth, where Terry Alderman damaged his shoulder badly when he rugby-tackled a football hooligan who had somehow found his way on to the cricket field. Alderman could take no further part, but we were comprehensively beaten at Brisbane, where Kepler Wessels, later to lead South Africa back into international cricket, scored a big hundred in his first Test for Australia. This had been followed by the ignominy of Adelaide where I was daft enough to put Australia in after consulting my senior batsmen, Gower, Lamb and Botham, none of whom wanted to bat first on a flat pitch. I think it was my weakest moment as captain and one which I will never be allowed to forget. Ian Chappell, among others, is always very happy to remind me about what happened at the Adelaide Oval when England invited Australia to bat first and were slaughtered by eight wickets.

Melbourne was a different story. We had a team meeting at the Hilton Hotel where Beefy and Lamby had clearly taken wine, as they say, and turned up in a much more positive frame of mind. The guys who did not want to bat at Adelaide were saying that it was no good just going out to occupy the crease; we had to be more dominant and try to take on the Australian bowlers in a way which we had not been able to do in the previous matches. This time Australia put us in to bat and we really got stuck into them. They led us by three runs after the first innings, but we set them 292 to win which was always going to take some getting with Norman Cowans bowling very well and troubling Test batsmen with his pace for just about the only time in his international career. Crucially, Greg Chappell was going through the horrors against the short-pitched ball and Norman picked him up for 0 and 2. By the fourth afternoon, we had got ourselves into an almost unassailable position with the Australians still needing another 74 with only one wicket left.

It was then that Jeff Thomson joined Allan Border and I quickly adopted the tactic of trying to bowl at Thomson as much as we could by giving Border the single. The trouble was that Border did not just play quite superbly himself, but he also convinced his Queensland colleague that it had become a very flat wicket and, by playing straight, he would survive easily enough. Border had effectively trumped my ace with his own tactics. He was quite happy to let Tommo take plenty of the strike, and slowly but surely the target got smaller and smaller. By the end of the day, they had got it down to 37 and when they continued in the same vein on the final morning to reduce it to a mere 4 I thought I had better pull my white rabbit out of the hat. I decided that if anything was going to get me that last wicket it was going to be the golden arm of Botham, and it did not let me down. Tommo immediately got an edge and the ball flew to second slip. Chris Tavare could only parry it into the air but Geoff Miller ran round behind him from first slip to take the catch and we all charged off the field to celebrate a very rare victory in a Test match away from home. It sent us into the last Test at Sydney believing that we could square the series but unfortunately the weather and an umpire called Mel Johnson had other ideas, the match petered out into a draw and Australia took the Ashes.

### ENGLAND

| | | |
|---|---|---|
| G. Cook c Chappell b Thomson .... | 0 – | c Yardley b Thomson .... 26 |
| G. Fowler c Chappell b Hogg ...... | 4 – | b Hogg ............... 65 |
| C. Tavare c Yardley b Thomson .... | 89 – | b Hogg ............... 0 |
| D. Gower c Marsh b Hogg ........ | 18 – | c Marsh b Lawson ....... 3 |
| A. Lamb c Dyson b Yardley ....... | 83 – | c Marsh b Hogg ........ 26 |
| I. Botham c Wessels b Yardley ..... | 27 – | c Chappell b Thomson ... 46 |
| G. Miller c Border b Yardley ...... | 10 – | lbw Lawson ........... 14 |
| D. Pringle c Wessels b Hogg ....... | 9 – | c Marsh b Lawson ....... 42 |
| R. Taylor c Marsh b Yardley ....... | 1 – | lbw Thompson ......... 37 |
| R. Willis not out ............... | 6 – | not out .............. 8 |
| N. Cowans c Lawson b Hogg ...... | 3 – | b Lawson ............. 10 |
| Extras (b3, lb6, w3, nb12) ...... | 24 – | (b2, lb9, nb6) ......... 17 |
| Total ................... | 284 | ...................294 |

1–11, 2–25, 3–56, 4–217, 5–227, 6–259, 7–262, 8–268, 9–278
1–40, 2–41, 3–45, 4–128, 5–129, 6–160, 7–201, 8–262, 9–280

| | | | | | | | | |
|---|---|---|---|---|---|---|---|---|
| Lawson | 17 | 6 | 48 | 0 | 21.4 | 6 | 66 | 4 |
| Hogg | 22.3 | 6 | 69 | 4 | 22 | 5 | 64 | 3 |
| Yardley | 27 | 9 | 89 | 4 | 15 | 2 | 67 | 0 |
| Thomson | 13 | 2 | 49 | 2 | 21 | 3 | 74 | 3 |
| Chappell | 1 | 0 | 5 | 0 | 1 | 0 | 6 | 0 |

## AUSTRALIA

K. Wessels b Willis .............. 47 – b Cowans ............. 14
J. Dyson lbw Cowans ........... 21 – c Tavare b Botham ...... 31
G. Chappell c Lamb b Cowans ..... 0 – c sub (Gould) b Cowans .. 2
K. Hughes b Willis .............. 66 – c Taylor b Miller ....... 48
A. Border b Botham ............ 2 – not out .............. 62
D. Hookes c Taylor b Pringle ...... 53 – c Willis b Cowans ....... 68
R. Marsh b Willis .............. 53 – lbw Cowans ........... 13
B. Yardley b Miller ............ 9 – b Cowans ............. 0
G. Lawson c Fowler b Miller ....... 0 – c Cowans b Pringle ...... 7
R. Hogg not out ................ 8 – lbw Cowans ........... 4
J. Thomson b Miller ........... 1 – c Miller b Botham ...... 21
  Extras (lb8, nb19) ............. 27 – (b5, lb9, w1, nb3) ....... 18

  Total ................. 287 .................... 288

1–55, 2–55, 3–83, 4–89, 5–180, 6–261, 7–276, 8–276, 9–278
1–37, 2–39, 3–71, 4–171, 5–173, 6–190, 7–190, 8–202, 9–218

| | | | | | | | | |
|---|---|---|---|---|---|---|---|---|
| Willis  | 15 | 2 | 38 | 3 | 17   | 0 | 57 | 0 |
| Botham  | 18 | 3 | 69 | 1 | 25.1 | 4 | 80 | 2 |
| Cowans  | 16 | 0 | 69 | 2 | 26   | 6 | 77 | 6 |
| Pringle | 15 | 2 | 40 | 1 | 12   | 4 | 26 | 1 |
| Miller  | 15 | 5 | 44 | 3 | 16   | 6 | 30 | 1 |

# 4: Madras, 1986–7

*Australia won toss. India tied with Australia.*
Greg Matthews pinned Maninder Singh lbw with the last but one
ball of the match to produce only the second tie in the history of
Test cricket. Australia had also been involved in the other one –
against the West Indies at Brisbane in 1960–1 when Ian Meckiff
was run out off the penultimate delivery. That was always a close-
run thing, but no one foresaw the possibility of it happening again
when Australia were piling up a first innings total of 574 for 7
declared, their highest score on Indian soil. David Boon and Allan
Border both made centuries but the real hero was Dean Jones who
battled through bouts of sickness and cramp for nearly eight and a
half hours in the heat and humidity to make 210, and finished up
in hospital on a saline drip.

Krish Srikkanth and Mohammad Azharuddin responded with
aggressive fifties and Ravi Shastri batted more sedately for 62, but
India looked like having to follow on until their captain, Kapil Dev,

smashed a century off only 109 balls. Australia were still looking for victory when they set India 348 to win in a minimum of eighty-seven overs on the final morning, but they had reckoned without the great Sunil Gavaskar, playing in his hundredth consecutive Test match. He had been involved in some famous run chases in his time, most notably at Port-of-Spain in 1975–6 when India scored 406 for 4 to beat the West Indies and at The Oval in 1979 when they got within nine runs of making 438 to beat England. Now he timed his effort so well that India reached the final twenty overs needing only 118 with seven wickets in hand against a tiring Australian attack which was very much on the defensive. They had reached 251 when Gavaskar mistimed a cover drive and was out for 90, and although Kapil went two runs later, Azharuddin and Shastri seemed to have the job well under control. Even after Azharuddin was out, it did not appear to be a problem with eighteen wanted off thirty balls, and four wickets left, but then Ray Bright took two wickets in one over to set up an unbelievable climax.

Shivlal Yadav, having smashed Matthews for six, was bowled off his pads by Bright, and Maninder had to survive two balls before Shastri faced the final over from Matthews with just four wanted. He got two off the second ball, helped by a misfield, and then chose to take a single off the third which meant that India could not lose, but left Maninder, one of the game's great rabbits, to win the game for them. It was beyond him. He only just managed to survive the fourth ball and was out to the fifth, giving Matthews his tenth wicket of the match and the frenzied 30,000 crowd a finish they will never forget.

## AUSTRALIA

| | | | |
|---|---|---|---|
| D. Boon c Kapil Dev b Chetan | 122 – | lbw Maninder | 49 |
| G. Marsh c Kapil Dev b Yadav | 22 – | b Shastri | 11 |
| D. Jones b Yadav | 210 – | c Azharuddin b Maninder | 24 |
| R. Bright c Shastri b Yadav | 30 – | | |
| A. Border c Gavaskar b Shastri | 106 – | b Maninder | 27 |
| G. Ritchie run out | 13 – | c Pandit b Shastri | 28 |
| G. Matthews c Pandit b Yadav | 44 – | not out | 27 |
| S. Waugh not out | 12 – | not out | 2 |
| Extras (b1, lb7, w1, nb6) | 15 – | (lb1, nb1) | 2 |
| Total (7 wickets dec.) | 574 | (5 wickets dec.) | 170 |

1–48, 2–206, 3–282, 4–460, 5–481, 6–544, 7–574
1–31, 2–81, 3–94, 4–125, 5–165

| | | | | | | | | |
|---|---|---|---|---|---|---|---|---|
| Kapil Dev | 18 | 5 | 52 | 0 | 1 | 0 | 5 | 0 |
| Chetan | 16 | 1 | 70 | 1 | 6 | 0 | 19 | 0 |
| Maninder | 39 | 8 | 135 | 0 | 19 | 2 | 60 | 3 |
| Yadav | 49.5 | 9 | 142 | 4 | 9 | 0 | 35 | 0 |
| Shastri | 47 | 8 | 161 | 1 | 14 | 2 | 50 | 2 |

## INDIA

| | | | |
|---|---|---|---|
| S. Gavaskar c and b Matthews | 8 | – c Jones b Bright | 90 |
| K. Srikkanth c Ritchie b Matthews | 53 | – c Waugh b Matthews | 39 |
| M. Amarnath run out | 1 | – c Boon b Matthews | 51 |
| M. Azharuddin c and b Bright | 50 | – c Ritchie b Bright | 42 |
| R. Shastri c Zoehrer b Matthews | 62 | – not out | 48 |
| C. Pandit c Waugh b Matthews | 35 | – b Matthews | 39 |
| Kapil Dev c Border b Matthews | 119 | – c Bright b Matthews | 1 |
| K. More c Zoehrer b Waugh | 4 | – lbw Bright | 0 |
| Chetan Sharma c Zoehrer b Reid | 30 | – c McDermott b Bright | 23 |
| S. Yadav c Border b Bright | 19 | – b Bright | 8 |
| Maninder Singh not out | 0 | – lbw Matthews | 0 |
| Extras (b1, lb9, nb6) | 16 | – (b1, lb3, nb2) | 6 |
| Total | 397 | | 347 |

1–62, 2–65, 3–65, 4–142, 5–206, 6–220, 7–245, 8–330, 9–387
1–55, 2–158, 3–204, 4–251, 5–253, 6–291, 7–331, 8–334, 9–344

| | | | | | | | | |
|---|---|---|---|---|---|---|---|---|
| McDermott | 14 | 2 | 59 | 0 | 5 | 0 | 27 | 0 |
| Reid | 18 | 4 | 93 | 1 | 10 | 2 | 48 | 0 |
| Matthews | 28.2 | 3 | 103 | 5 | 39.5 | 7 | 146 | 5 |
| Bright | 23 | 8 | 88 | 2 | 25 | 3 | 94 | 5 |
| Waugh | 11 | 2 | 44 | 1 | 4 | 1 | 16 | 0 |
| Border | | | | | 3 | 0 | 12 | 0 |

## 5: Christchurch, 1991–2

*New Zealand won toss. England won by an innings and four runs.*
It is not often that a Test match which finishes in an innings victory
can be described as exciting but this one was. There were only ten
minutes left when New Zealand's captain, Martin Crowe, going
for the shot which would have levelled the scores and ensured a
draw, skied Phil Tufnell to mid-off and gave England a win that
had seemed beyond them. England had been dictating the game
almost from the moment that Crowe put them in on a slow pitch.
Graham Gooch fell cheaply to Danny Morrison but Alec Stewart
more than made up for that by playing better than he had ever done
in a Test match. It was not so much his strokeplay as his control
which caught the eye as he batted for most of the first day for 148,
and with Robin Smith, Allan Lamb, Chris Lewis and Dermot
Reeve, on his Test debut, all playing well, England reached 580 for
9 declared.

The only question after that was whether England could bowl
New Zealand out twice in the time remaining and their chances
were reduced when bad light wiped out most of the second evening
and all of the third morning. It all depended on Tufnell, bowling
as well as he has ever done for England, and he raised their hopes
by taking four of New Zealand's first five wickets for twenty. They
were 139 for 6 when Crowe fell to Derek Pringle, but England's
hopes of enforcing the follow-on were threatened when Dipak Patel
and Chris Cairns hit back with a seventh-wicket stand of 117. Patel
was within one run of a maiden Test century when he took the
liberty of risking a third run to Pringle as he caught up with the ball
at long-on and was run out by a yard. New Zealand were batting
again before tea on the fourth day but by tea on the fifth England
still had to take seven more wickets with only fifty-seven runs to
play with.

It was then that Tufnell showed what a match-winner he can be.
John Wright finally ran out of patience after over six hours and was
stumped for 99, Mark Greatbatch and Shane Thomson were out in
the same over and Patel and Cairns soon followed. When Lewis
chipped in to get rid of Ian Smith, Crowe and Chris Pringle had half
an hour to survive or eighteen runs to make. They had got fourteen
of them in twenty minutes when Crowe gambled everything against
a teasing delivery from Tufnell and lost. England had won their third
Test match in a row and Tufnell had taken five wickets or more in
an innings in each of them. Would that it happened more often.

## ENGLAND

G. Gooch c Smith b Morrison . . . . . .     2
A. Stewart c Crowe b Morrison . . . . .   148
G. Hick lbw Cairns . . . . . . . . . . . . . .    35
R. Smith c Greatbatch b Pringle   . . . .    96
A. Lamb b Patel . . . . . . . . . . . . . . .    93
J.  Russell run out . . . . . . . . . . . . . . .    36
D. Reeve c Jones b Pringle  . . . . . . . .    59
C. Lewis b Pringle  . . . . . . . . . . . . . .    70
D. Pringle c Greatbatch b Patel  . . . . .    10
P. DeFreitas not out  . . . . . . . . . . . . .     7
    Extras (b5, lb10, w1, nb8) . . . . . . .    24

    Total   (9 wickets dec.) . . . . . . . . .   580

1–6, 2–95, 3–274, 4–310, 5–390, 6–466, 7–544, 8–571, 9–580

| Morrison | 33 | 5 | 133 | 2 |
|---|---|---|---|---|
| Cairns | 30 | 3 | 118 | 1 |
| Pringle | 36 | 4 | 127 | 3 |
| Thomson | 15 | 3 | 47 | 0 |
| Patel | 46 | 5 | 132 | 2 |
| Jones | 3 | 0 | 8 | 0 |

## NEW ZEALAND

B. Hartland c Smith b Tufnell . . . . . .    22 – c Smith b Tufnell  . . . . . . .    45
J.  Wright c Lamb b Tufnell . . . . . . .    28 – st Russell b Tufnell . . . . . .    99
A. Jones lbw Lewis . . . . . . . . . . . . . .    16 – c Russell b Pringle  . . . . . .    39
M. Greatbatch c Stewart b Tufnell . . .    11 – c Smith b Tufnell  . . . . . . .     0
S.  Thomson b Tufnell . . . . . . . . . . . .     5 – lbw Tufnell . . . . . . . . . . . .     0
D. Patel run out . . . . . . . . . . . . . . . .    99 – c Pringle b Tufnell  . . . . . .     6
M. Crowe c Stewart b Pringle . . . . . .    20 – c Pringle b Tufnell  . . . . . .    48
C. Cairns c Hick b Reeve . . . . . . . . .    61 – c Smith b Tufnell  . . . . . . .     0
I.  Smith lbw DeFreitas . . . . . . . . . . .    20 – c Russell b Lewis  . . . . . . .     1
D. Morrison not out . . . . . . . . . . . . .     8 – c Russell b Lewis  . . . . . . .     0
C. Pringle c Hick b DeFreitas . . . . . .     6 – not out . . . . . . . . . . . . . . .     5
    Extras  (b1, lb7, nb8) . . . . . . . . . .    16 – (b1, lb7, nb13) . . . . . . . . .    21

    Total . . . . . . . . . . . . . . . . . . . . . .   312     . . . . . . . . . . . . . . . . . . . . .264

1–51, 2–52, 3–73, 4–87, 5–91, 6–139, 7–256, 8–279, 9–306
1–81, 2–81, 3–182, 4–211, 5–222, 6–222, 7–236, 8–241, 9–250

| DeFreitas | 32.4 | 16 | 54 | 2 | 23 | 6 | 54 | 0 |
|---|---|---|---|---|---|---|---|---|
| Lewis | 30 | 9 | 69 | 1 | 22 | 3 | 66 | 2 |
| Pringle | 15 | 2 | 54 | 1 | 21 | 5 | 64 | 1 |
| Tufnell | 39 | 10 | 100 | 4 | 46.1 | 25 | 47 | 7 |
| Hick | 3 | 0 | 11 | 0 | 14 | 8 | 11 | 0 |
| Reeve | 8 | 4 | 16 | 1 | 2 | 0 | 8 | 0 |
| Smith | | | | | 4 | 2 | 6 | 0 |

## 6: Adelaide, 1992–3

*West Indies won toss. West Indies beat Australia by one run.*
'What can you say – one run?' asked Australia's captain, Allan Border, after the West Indies had beaten them by the narrowest margin in 116 years of Test match cricket. Curtly Ambrose was the West Indies' match-winner with six wickets in Australia's first innings and four more in the second, including a burst of three wickets in nineteen balls just when it mattered most. Yet it was Courtney Walsh who clinched it when he got Craig McDermott to glove a lifting ball to wicketkeeper Junior Murray after he and Tim May had taken Australia within two runs of victory with a remarkable last-wicket stand of 40. It had been a compelling contest from the moment the West Indies batted first on a pitch that was juicier than usual at the Adelaide Oval because of recent rain. They got a decent start from Desmond Haynes and Phil Simmons but with the great-hearted Merv Hughes picking up five wickets they needed an unbeaten 49 from Murray to reach a total of 252.

Australia knew what they were up against when Ian Bishop got rid of Mark Taylor in his first over and then split Justin Langer's helmet with a delivery which had 'Welcome to Test cricket' written all over it. Next morning David Boon took a painful enough blow on the arm to force even him to retire hurt and although he returned later to finish unbeaten on 39, Australia needed gutsy efforts from Steve Waugh and big Merv to limit their deficit to 39.

Then it was the West Indies' turn to struggle. McDermott had them reeling at 65 for 4 and no sooner had Richie Richardson and Carl Hooper pulled things round with a stand of 59 than May picked up 5 for 9 in 6.5 overs. The last six wickets went down for twenty-two and Australia fancied their chances of scoring 186 to win until Ambrose undermined them. There were wickets for Benjamin, Bishop and Walsh as well, as they collapsed to 74 for 7. The determined Langer was still there, though, and it was he who inspired a fantastic fight-back. Shane Warne helped him put on twenty-eight and May, defying an injured hand, another forty-two before the last-wicket pair got together in that heroic stand which had just about everybody in Australia glued to their television sets. They were almost there when Walsh got the ball to lift from around off stump and umpire Darrell Hair judged that it had brushed McDermott's glove on its way to Murray. Two more runs and Australia would have won the series. As it was, Ambrose blew them away in the final Test at Perth with an incredible spell of 7 for 1 in thirty-two balls and the West Indies took it 2–1.

## WEST INDIES

| | | | |
|---|---|---|---|
| D. Haynes st Healy b May | 45 | – c Healy b McDermott | 11 |
| P. Simmons c Hughes b S. Waugh | 46 | – b McDermott | 10 |
| R. Richardson lbw Hughes | 2 | – c Healy b Warne | 72 |
| B. Lara c Healy b McDermott | 52 | – c S. Waugh b Hughes | 7 |
| K. Arthurton c S. Waugh b May | 0 | – c Healy b McDermott | 0 |
| C. Hooper c Healy b Hughes | 2 | – c Hughes b May | 25 |
| J. Murray not out | 49 | – c M. Waugh b May | 0 |
| I. Bishop c M. Waugh b Hughes | 13 | – c M. Waugh b May | 6 |
| C. Ambrose c Healy b Hughes | 0 | – st Healy b May | 1 |
| K. Benjamin b M. Waugh | 15 | – c Warne b May | 0 |
| C. Walsh lbw Hughes | 5 | – not out | 0 |
| Extras (b11, lb12) | 23 | – (lb2, nb12) | 14 |
| Total | 252 | | 146 |

1–84, 2–99, 3–129, 4–130, 5–134, 6–189, 7–206, 8–206, 9–247
1–14, 2–49, 3–63, 4–65, 5–124, 6–137, 7–145, 8–146, 9–146

| | | | | | | | | |
|---|---|---|---|---|---|---|---|---|
| McDermott | 16 | 1 | 85 | 1 | 11 | 0 | 66 | 3 |
| Hughes | 21.3 | 3 | 64 | 5 | 13 | 1 | 43 | 1 |
| S. Waugh | 13 | 4 | 37 | 1 | 5 | 1 | 8 | 0 |
| May | 14 | 1 | 41 | 2 | 6.5 | 3 | 9 | 5 |
| Warne | 2 | 0 | 11 | 0 | 6 | 2 | 18 | 1 |
| M. Waugh | 1 | 0 | 3 | 1 | | | | |

## AUSTRALIA

| | | | |
|---|---|---|---|
| M. Taylor c Hooper b Bishop | 1 | – c Murray b Benjamin | 7 |
| D. Boon not out | 39 | – lbw Ambrose | 0 |
| J. Langer c Murray b Benjamin | 20 | – c Murray b Bishop | 54 |
| M. Waugh c Simmons b Ambrose | 0 | – c Hooper b Walsh | 26 |
| S. Waugh c Murray b Ambrose | 42 | – c Arthurton b Ambrose | 4 |
| A. Border c Hooper b Ambrose | 19 | – c Haynes b Ambrose | 1 |
| I. Healy c Hooper b Ambrose | 0 | – b Walsh | 0 |
| M. Hughes c Murray b Hooper | 43 | – lbw Ambrose | 1 |
| S. Warne lbw Hooper | 0 | – lbw Bishop | 9 |
| T. May c Murray b Ambrose | 6 | – not out | 42 |
| C. McDermott b Ambrose | 14 | – c Murray b Walsh | 18 |
| Extras (b7, lb3, nb19) | 29 | – (b1, lb8, nb13) | 22 |
| Total | 213 | | 184 |

1–1, 2–16, 3–46, 4–108, 5–108, 6–112, 7–181, 8–181, 9–197
1–5, 2–16, 3–54, 4–64, 5–72, 6–73, 7–74, 8–102, 9–144

| | | | | | | | | |
|---|---|---|---|---|---|---|---|---|
| Ambrose | 28.2 | 6 | 74 | 6 | 26 | 5 | 46 | 4 |
| Bishop | 18 | 3 | 48 | 1 | 17 | 3 | 41 | 2 |
| Benjamin | 6 | 0 | 22 | 1 | 12 | 2 | 32 | 1 |
| Walsh | 10 | 3 | 34 | 0 | 19 | 4 | 44 | 3 |
| Hooper | 13 | 4 | 25 | 2 | 5 | 1 | 12 | 0 |

# GLOSSARY

Where overseas Test cricketers have played first-class cricket in England, the counties for which they played have been included. The cut-off date for the number of caps attributed to players is 1 March 1996.

Ahmed Mushtaq (28 June 1970) Somerset, 18 Pakistan caps.

Ahmed Tauseef (10 May 1958) 34 Pakistan caps.

Akram Wasim (3 June 1966) Lancashire, 67 Pakistan caps.

Alam Intikhab (28 December 1941) Surrey, 47 Pakistan caps.

Alderman Terry (12 June 1956) Kent and Gloucestershire, 41 Australia caps.

Allott Paul (14 September 1956) Lancashire, 13 England caps.

Ambrose Curtly (21 September 1963) Northants, 56 West Indies caps.

Ames Les (3 December 1905, died 26 February 1990) Kent, 47 England caps.

Amiss Dennis (7 April 1943) Warwickshire, 50 England caps.

Archer David (20 August 1931, died 24 October 1992) umpire.

Arnold Geoff (3 September 1944) Surrey and Sussex, 34 England caps.

Arthurton Keith (21 February 1965) 33 West Indies caps.

Atherton Michael (23 March 1968) Lancashire, 56 England caps.

Athey Bill (27 September 1957) Yorkshire, Gloucestershire and Sussex, 23 England caps.

Azharuddin Mohammad (8 February 1963) Derbyshire, 68 India caps.

Bailey Trevor (3 December 1923) Essex, 61 England caps.

Bairstow David (1 September 1951) Yorkshire, 4 England caps.

Bari Wasim (23 March 1948) 81 Pakistan caps.

Barlow Eddie (12 August 1940) Derbyshire, 30 South Africa caps.

Barlow Graham (26 March 1950) Middlesex, 3 England caps.

Barnes Sydney (19 April 1873, died 26 December 1967) Warwickshire and Lancashire, 27 England caps.

Barrington Ken (24 November 1930, died 14 March 1981) Surrey, 82 England caps.

Bedi Bishen (25 September 1946) Northamptonshire, 67 India caps.

Bedser Alec (4 July 1918) Surrey, 51 England caps.

Benjamin Kenny (8 April 1967) Worcestershire, 21 West Indies caps.

Bird Dickie (19 April 1933) Yorkshire and Leicestershire, umpire.

Blakey Richard (15 January 1967) Yorkshire, 2 England caps.

Bland Colin (5 April 1938) 21 South Africa caps.

Boock Stephen (20 September 1951) 30 New Zealand caps.

Border Allan (27 July 1955) Gloucestershire and Essex, 156 Australia caps.

Botham Ian (24 November 1955) Somerset, Worcestershire and Durham, 102 England caps.

Boycott Geoff (21 October 1940) Yorkshire, 108 England caps.

Bracewell John (15 April 1958) 41 New Zealand caps.

Bradman Sir Donald (27 August 1908) 52 Australia caps.

Brearley Mike (28 April 1942) Middlesex, 39 England caps.

Broad Chris (29 September 1957) Gloucestershire and Nottinghamshire, 25 England caps.

Bucknor Steve (31 May 1946) umpire.

Cairns Lance (10 October 1949) 43 New Zealand caps.

Capel David (6 February 1963) Northamptonshire, 15 England caps.

Chandrasekhar Bhagwat (17 May 1945) 58 India caps.

Chappell Greg (7 August 1948) Somerset, 87 Australia caps.

Chappell Ian (26 September 1943) Lancashire, 75 Australia caps.

Chatfield Ewan (3 July 1950) 43 New Zealand caps.

Close Brian (24 February 1931) Yorkshire and Somerset, 22 England caps.

Collinge Dick (2 April 1946) 35 New Zealand caps.

Compton Denis (23 May 1918) Middlesex, 78 England caps.

Cook Nick (17 June 1956) Leicestershire and Northamptonshire, 15 England caps.

Cork Dominic (7 August 1971) Derbyshire, 10 England caps.

Cottam Bob (16 October 1944) Hampshire and Northamptonshire, 4 England caps.

Cowans Norman (17 April 1961) Middlesex and Hampshire, 19 England caps.

Cowdrey Colin (24 December 1932) Kent, 114 England caps.

Croft Colin (15 March 1953) Lancashire, 75 West Indies caps.

Crowe Martin (22 September 1962) Somerset, 74 New Zealand caps.

Davidson Alan (14 June 1929) 44 Australia caps.

DeFreitas Phillip (18 February 1966) Leicestershire, Lancashire and Derbyshire, 44 England caps.

Dev Kapil (6 January 1959) Northamptonshire and Worcestershire, 131 India caps.

Dexter Ted (15 May 1935) Sussex, 62 England caps.

Dilley Graham (18 May 1959) Kent and Worcestershire, 41 England caps.

D'Oliveira Basil (4 October 1931) Worcestershire, 44 England caps.

Donald Allan (20 October 1966) Warwickshire, 25 South Africa caps.

Downton Paul (4 April 1957) Kent and Middlesex, 30 England caps.

Dujon Jeff (28 May 1956) 81 West Indies caps.

Dymock Geoff (21 July 1945) 21 Australia caps.

Edmonds Phil (8 March 1951) Middlesex, 51 England caps.

Edrich John (21 June 1937) Surrey, 77 England caps.

Ehtesham-ud-Din (4 September 1950) 5 Pakistan caps.

Elliott Charlie (24 April 1912) Derbyshire umpire.

Ellison Richard (21 September 1959) Kent, 11 England caps.

Emburey John (20 August 1952) Middlesex, 64 England caps.

Engineer Farokh (25 February 1938) Lancashire, 46 India caps.

Evans Godfrey (18 August 1920) Kent, 91 England caps.

Fairbrother Neil (9 September 1963) Lancashire, 10 England caps.

Fleming Damien (24 April 1970) 4 Australia caps.

Fletcher Keith (20 May 1944) Essex, 59 England caps.

Flower Andy (28 April 1968) 16 Zimbabwe caps.

Foster Neil (6 May 1962) Essex, 29 England caps.

Fraser Angus (8 August 1965) Middlesex, 32 England caps.

Fredericks Roy (11 November 1942) Glamorgan, 59 West Indies caps.

French Bruce (13 August 1959) Nottinghamshire, 16 England caps.

Gallian Jason (25 June 1971) Lancashire, 3 England caps.

Garner Joel (16 December 1952) Somerset, 58 West Indies caps.

Gatting Mike (6 June 1957) Middlesex, 79 England caps.

Gavaskar Sunil (10 July 1949) Somerset, 125 India caps.

Gibbs Lance (29 September 1934) Warwickshire, 79 West Indies caps.

Gilmour Gary (26 June 1951) 15 Australia caps.

Gooch Graham (23 July 1952) Essex, 118 England caps.

Gough Darren (18 September 1970) Yorkshire, 12 England caps.

Gould Ian (19 August 1957) Middlesex and Sussex.

Gower David (1 April 1957) Leicestershire and Hampshire, 117
    England caps.

Greenidge Gordon (26 May 1948) Sussex, 108 West Indies caps.

Greig Ian (8 December 1955) Sussex and Surrey, 2 England caps.

Greig Tony (6 October 1946) Sussex, 58 England caps.

Grimmett Clarrie (25 December 1891, died 2 May 1980) 37 Australia caps.

Hadlee Sir Richard (3 July 1951) Nottinghamshire, 86 New Zealand caps.

Hammond Walter (19 June 1903, died 1 July 1965) Gloucestershire, 85 England caps.

Hampshire John (10 February 1941) Yorkshire and Derbyshire, 8 England caps.

Harper Roger (17 March 1963) Northamptonshire, 25 West Indies caps.

Harvey Neil (8 October 1928) 79 Australia caps.

Haynes Desmond (15 February 1956) Middlesex, 116 West Indies caps.

Headley George (30 May 1909, died 30 November 1983) 22 West Indies caps.

Healy Ian (30 April 1964) 73 Australia caps.

Hemmings Eddie (20 February 1949) Warwickshire, Nottinghamshire and Sussex, 16 England caps.

Hendrick Mike (22 October 1948) Derbyshire and Nottinghamshire, 30 England caps.

Hick Graeme (23 May 1966) Worcestershire, 42 England caps.

Higgs Jim (11 July 1950) 22 Australia caps.

Hirwani Narendra (18 October 1968) 14 India caps.

Hobbs Sir Jack (16 December 1882, died 21 December 1963) Surrey, 61 England caps.

Michael Holding (16 February 1954) Lancashire and Derbyshire, 60 West Indies caps.

Howarth Geoff (29 March 1951) Surrey, 47 New Zealand caps.

Humpage Geoff (24 April 1954) Warwickshire.

Hurst Alan (15 July 1950) 12 Australia caps.

Hussain Nasser (28 March 1968) Essex, 7 England caps.

Hutton Sir Len (23 June 1916, died 6 September 1990) Yorkshire, 79 England caps.

Hutton Richard (6 September 1942) Yorkshire, 5 England caps.

Igglesden Alan (8 October 1964) Kent, 3 England caps.

Illingworth Ray (8 June 1932) Yorkshire and Leicestershire, 61 England caps.

Illingworth Richard (23 August 1963) Worcestershire, 6 England caps.

Ilott Mark (27 August 1970) Essex, 3 England caps.

Iqbal Asif (6 June 1943) Kent, 58 Pakistan caps.

Jackman Robin (13 August 1945) Surrey, 4 England caps.

Johnston Bill (26 February 1922) 40 Australia caps.

Julien Bernard (13 March 1950) Kent, 24 West Indies caps.

Kallicharran Alvin (21 March 1949) Warwickshire, 66 West Indies caps.

Kanhai Rohan (26 December 1935) Warwickshire, 79 West Indies caps.

Khan Imran (25 November 1952) Worcestershire and Sussex, 88 Pakistan caps.

Khan Majid (28 September 1946) Glamorgan, 63 Pakistan caps.

Kirmani Syed (29 December 1949) 88 India caps.

Kishen Swaroop (13 July 1930), umpire.

Knott Alan (9 April 1946) Kent, 95 England caps.

Kumble Anil (17 October 1970) Northamptonshire, 23 India caps.

Laker Jim (9 February 1922, died 23 April 1986) Surrey and Essex, 46 England caps.

Lal Madan (20 March 1951) 39 India caps.

Lamb Allan (20 June 1954) Northamptonshire, 79 England caps.

Lara Brian (2 May 1969) Warwickshire, 31 West Indies caps.

Larkins Wayne (22 November 1953) Northamptonshire and Durham, 13 England caps.

Larwood Harold (14 November 1904, died 22 July 1995) Nottinghamshire, 21 England caps.

Lever John (24 February 1949) Essex, 21 England caps.

Lever Peter (17 September 1940) Lancashire, 17 England caps.

Lewis Chris (14 February 1968) Leicestershire and Nottinghamshire, 27 England caps.

Lillee Dennis (18 July 1949) Northamptonshire, 70 Australia caps.

Lloyd Clive (31 August 1944) Lancashire, 110 West Indies caps.

Lloyd David (18 March 1947) Lancashire, 9 England caps.

Lock Tony (5 July 1929, died 29 March 1995) Surrey and Leicestershire, 49 England caps.

Logie Gus (28 September 1960) 52 West Indies caps.

Luckhurst Brian (5 February 1939) Kent, 21 England caps.

Mahmood Fazal (18 February 1927) 34 Pakistan caps.

Malcolm Devon (22 February 1963) Derbyshire, 34 England caps.

Mallett Ashley (13 July 1945) 38 Australia caps.

Marsh Geoff (31 December 1958) 50 Australia caps.

Marsh Rodney (4 November 1947) 96 Australia caps.

Marshall Malcolm (18 April 1958) Hampshire, 81 West Indies caps.

Massie Bob (14 April 1947) 6 Australia caps.

May Peter (31 December 1929, died 27 December 1994) Surrey, 66 England caps.

May Tim (26 January 1962) 24 Australia caps.

McCague Martin (24 May 1969) Kent, 3 England caps.

McDermott Craig (14 April 1965) 71 Australia caps.

McGrath Glenn (9 February 1970) 19 Australia caps.

McKenzie Graham (24 June 1941) Leicestershire, 60 Australia caps.

McMillan Brian (22 December 1963) Warwickshire, 23 South Africa caps.

Metson Colin (2 July 1963) Middlesex and Glamorgan.

Meyer Barrie (21 August 1932) Gloucestershire, umpire.

Miandad Javed (12 June 1957) Sussex and Glamorgan, 124 Pakistan caps.

Miller Geoff (8 September 1952) Derbyshire and Essex, 34 England caps.

Miller Keith (28 November 1919) Nottinghamshire, 55 Australia caps.

Mohammad Hanif (21 December 1934) 55 Pakistan caps.

Mohammad Mushtaq (22 November 1943) Northamptonshire, 57 Pakistan caps.

More Kieron (4 September 1962) 49 India caps.

Morris Arthur (19 January 1922) 46 Australia caps.

Morris Hugh (5 October 1963) Glamorgan, 3 England caps.

Murray Deryck (20 May 1943) Nottinghamshire and Warwickshire, 62 West Indies caps.

Murray John (1 April 1935) Middlesex, 21 England caps.

Nazar Mudassar (6 April 1956) 76 Pakistan caps.

Newport Phil (11 October 1962) Worcestershire, 3 England caps.

O'Reilly Bill (20 December 1905, died 6 October 1992) 27 Australia caps.

Old Chris (22 December 1948) Yorkshire and Warwickshire, 46 England caps.

Parks Jim (21 October 1931) Sussex and Somerset, 46 England caps.

Parore Adam (23 January 1971) 26 New Zealand caps.

Piper Keith (18 December 1969) Warwickshire.

Pocock Pat (24 September 1946) Surrey, 25 England caps.

Pollock Graeme (27 February 1944) 28 South Africa caps.

Ponsford Bill (19 October 1900, died 6 April 1991) 29 Australia caps.

Prasanna Erapally (22 May 1940) 49 India caps.

Price John (22 July 1937) Middlesex, 15 England caps.

Pringle Derek (18 September 1958) Essex, 30 England caps.

Procter Mike (15 September 1946) Gloucestershire, 7 South Africa caps.

Qadir Abdul (15 September 1955) 67 Pakistan caps.

Qasim Iqbal (6 August 1953) 50 Pakistan caps.

Raja Wasim (3 July 1952) 57 Pakistan caps.

Raju Venkatapathy (9 July 1969) 23 India caps.

Ramprakash Mark (5 September 1969) Middlesex, 19 England caps.

Randall Derek (24 February 1951) Nottinghamshire, 47 England caps.

Reid Bruce (14 March 1963) 27 Australia caps.

Reiffel Paul (19 April 1966) 16 Australia caps.

Rhodes Jonty (26 July 1969) 27 South Africa caps.

Rhodes Steve (17 June 1964) Yorkshire and Worcestershire, 11 England caps.

Rhodes Wilfred (29 October 1877, died 8 July 1973) Yorkshire, 58 England caps.

Richards Barry (21 July 1945) Gloucestershire and Hampshire, 4 South Africa caps.

Richards Jack (10 August 1958) Surrey, 8 England caps.

Richards Viv (7 March 1952) Somerset and Glamorgan, 121 West Indies caps.

Richardson David (16 September 1959) 28 South Africa caps.

Roberts Andy (29 January 1951) Hampshire, Leicestershire, 47 West Indies caps.

Robinson Tim (21 November 1958) Nottinghamshire, 29 England caps.

Roope Graham (12 July 1946) Surrey, 21 England caps.

Rowan Lou  (2 May 1925) umpire.

Rowe Lawrence (8 January 1949) Derbyshire, 30 West Indies caps.

Russell Jack (15 August 1963) Gloucestershire, 44 England caps.

Salisbury Ian (21 January 1970) Sussex, 7 England caps.

Sang Hue Douglas, umpire.

Selvey Mike (25 April 1948) Surrey, Middlesex and Glamorgan, 3
England caps.

Sharpe Phil (27 December 1936) Yorkshire and Derbyshire, 12 England
caps.

Shastri Ravi (27 May 1962) Glamorgan, 80 India caps.

Shepherd David (27 December 1940) Gloucestershire, umpire.

Shuttleworth Ken (13 November 1944) Lancashire and Leicestershire, 5
England caps.

Simpson Bob (3 February 1936) 62 Australia caps.

Singh Maninder (13 June 1965) 35 India caps.

Slater Michael (21 February 1970) 27 Australia caps.

Small Gladstone (18 October 1961) Warwickshire, 17 England caps.

Smith Ian (28 February 1957) 63 New Zealand caps.

Smith Robin (13 September 1963) Hampshire, 57 England caps.

Snow John (13 October 1941) Sussex, 49 England caps.

Sobers Sir Garfield (28 July 1936) Nottinghamshire, 93 West Indies
caps.

Sohail Aamir (14 September 1966) 30 Pakistan caps.

Solkar Eknath (18 March 1948) Sussex, 27 India caps.

Srinath Javagal (31 August 1969) 15 India caps.

Statham Brian (17 June 1930) Lancashire, 70 England caps.

Steele David (29 September 1941) Northamptonshire and Derbyshire, 8
England caps.

Stewart Alec (8 April 1963) Surrey, 53 England caps.

Such Peter (12 June 1964) Nottinghamshire, Leicestershire and Essex, 8
England caps.

Sutcliffe Herbert (24 November 1894, died 22 January 1978) Yorkshire, 54 England caps.

Tate Maurice (30 May 1985, died 18 May 1956) Sussex, 39 England caps.

Tavare Chris (27 October 1954) Kent and Somerset, 31 England caps.

Taylor Bob (17 July 1941) Derbyshire, 57 England caps.

Taylor Les (25 October 1953) Leicestershire, 2 England caps.

Taylor Mark (27 October 1964) 66 Australia caps.

Thomas Greg (12 August 1960) Glamorgan and Northamptonshire, 5 England caps.

Thomson Jeff (16 August 1950) Middlesex, 51 Australia caps.

Thorpe Graham (1 August 1969) Surrey, 26 England caps.

Titmus Fred (24 November 1932) Middlesex and Surrey, 53 England caps.

Tolchard Roger (15 June 1946) Leicestershire, 4 England caps.

Trueman Fred (6 February 1931) Yorkshire, 67 England caps.

Tufnell Phil (29 April 1966) Middlesex, 22 England caps.

Turner Glenn (26 May 1947) Worcestershire, 41 New Zealand caps.

Tyson Frank (6 June 1930) Northamptonshire, 17 England caps.

Underwood Derek (8 June 1945) Kent, 86 England caps.

Venkataraghavan Srinivas (21 April 1946) Derbyshire, 57 India caps, umpire.

Verity Hedley (18 May 1905, died 31 July 1943) Yorkshire, 40 England caps.

Wadsworth Ken (30 November 1946, died 19 August 1976) 33 New Zealand caps.

Walker Max (12 September 1948) 34 Australia caps.

Walsh Courtney (30 October 1962) Gloucestershire, 80 West Indies caps.

Walters Doug (21 December 1945) 74 Australia caps.

Ward Alan (10 August 1947) Derbyshire and Leicestershire, 5 England caps.

Wardle Johnny (8 January 1923, died 23 July 1985) Yorkshire, 28 England caps.

Warne Shane (13 September 1969) 44 Australia caps.

Washbrook Cyril (6 December 1914) Lancashire, 37 England caps.

Watkinson Mike (1 August 1961) Lancashire, 4 England caps.

Waugh Mark (2 June 1965) Essex, 54 Australia caps.

Waugh Steve (2 June 1965) Somerset, 81 Australia caps.

Weekes Everton (26 February 1925) 48 West Indies caps.

Whitehead Alan (28 October 1940) Somerset, umpire.

Willey Peter (6 December 1949) Northamptonshire and Leicestershire, 26 England caps, umpire.

Willis Bob (30 May 1949) Surrey and Warwickshire, 90 England caps.

Wood Barry (26 December 1942) Yorkshire, Lancashire and Derbyshire, 12 England caps.

Wright John (5 July 1954) Derbyshire, 82 New Zealand caps.

Yardley Bruce (5 September 1947) 33 Australia caps.

Younis Waqar (16 November 1971) Surrey, 38 Pakistan caps.